Window Fishing

Window Fishing

The night we caught Beatlemania

Selected and Edited by
John B. Lee

Second Edition

Hidden Brook Press
www.HiddenBrookPress.com
writers@HiddenBrookPress.com

Window Fishing: The night we caught Beatlemania

Editor – John B. Lee
Cover Photographer – unknown
Cover Design – Richard M. Grove
Layout and Design – Richard M. Grove

Typeset in Cambria

Printed and bound in USA

Library and Archives Canada Cataloguing in Publication

Window fishing : the night we caught Beatlemania / selected and edited by John B. Lee. -- 2nd edition.

ISBN 978-1-927725-14-6 (pbk.)

1. Beatles--Literary collections. 2. Canadian literature (English)--21st century. I. Lee, John B., 1951-, editor of compilation

PS8237.B42W55 2014 C810.8'0351 C2014-904722-3

for love of the music
for the next generation

and for my grandsons Talli, Teo and Cayden

Table of Contents

Encore ...

Window Fishing

"... a car and a room and a room and a car
and a car and a room and a cheese sandwich ..."

John Lennon's description of Beatlemania
as experienced by the Beatles

We were born in an age of assassins. Our childhood martyred almost all the heroes that we'd had. Forbidden means to desperate ends have stolen every voice we'd loved as best. When petty monsters took up guns and shot the poets of our youth, the papers mourned an old romance. Who knew a time would come to name the sudden dead as ours. I was but a callow baseball-playing lad when Miss Myrtle Downie closed the classroom door to tell us that America had murdered hope. And then we saw the film. We witnessed television horror come on Sunday to a Dallas basement jail. That was the wincing day when I turned twelve. Then Memphis woke us weeping with the news of fatal balconies. We'd grieved, we thought, enough, until we fell like kitchen dishes dropped from shock too great to bear. The brilliant brother broke upon the floor as well. The list is overlong. It will not end. My younger heart surrounds a tragic hour. I talk of fallen names. I nudge at corpses and am saddened by a private grief for public shame. Who killed these men killed innocence. I remember J.F.K. I remember Martin Luther King. I remember Robert F. Kennedy. I remember them all alive when lilacs last in the dooryard bloomed. I remember them well and fond and lost my adolescence blinking in their funeral smoke. That was the time the Beatles sang my life awake. Imagine that, this death of dream, with unanticipated mourning yet to come.

Editor
John B. Lee

1950s / 1960s

Robert Sward

Pre-med
thinking he's
got to learn about the world
all over again from
square one

Doesn't think he knows anything for sure
only Ed Sullivan and the Beatles,
the hula-hoops and Twinkies,
the blues and violets of his mind
very late at night

red and pink lipstick case
with a little mirror on one side,
hat, stockings, garter belt
and gloves

He bought a shirt in 1960 the most remarkable
feature of which is
that a snag or tear will reduce it
to nothing.

It's a shirt made of a single cell
that, when it's reduced to nothing,
a single cell remains.
The original cell of that fabric.

What he is seeking is a quilt
made up of the original cells of all the fabrics.

What the 1960s does
like a blow to the back or side of one's head
it relocates your mind

* * *

'Delicious' apples and the popularity of DDT

James Dean
Peter Lawford,
Elizabeth Taylor,
the Mickey Mouse Club,
taken seriously

The time many people who came into their own
in the 1960s
first got laid

The Rosenberg's frying in the electric chair
McCarthy and his crony Roy Cohn
the atomic bomb already five years old

Nixon: "California politics is a can of worms"
Ed Sullivan,
Captain Kangaroo, Howdy Doody
Strawberry fields forever,
Living is easy with eyes closed,
misunderstanding all you see.

* * *

Inhaling
The jazz was good
Death was softened, advancements made
in the salesmanship of everything

His own deepest impulses
were not to nurse or nurture
but to hang out again
at Sonny Berkowitz' Pool Hall,
wearing blue suede shoes,
Levis and navy blue shirt.
He bought a zip gun,
joined a street gang

Once, joint in hand,
exploring the intricacies
of the Chicago Drainage Canal,
he entered a sewer
and ambled deeply as he could

reflecting all the while
on his chances of surviving
the synchronized flushing
of three-and-a-half million toilets.

For the first time in 2,000 years
one went four years to a University
without hearing one true word;
going to work for Hallmark greeting cards
or the phone company
one knew something was at hand because things
became easy.
Tin-Pan alley
people in college dormitories subscribing
to Photoplay
and The Nail Polish Review.

Five foot two, eyes of blue,
cotton candy hair
fluffy lavender
angora sweater
short white socks
with fat cuffs
one of a hundred couples
in a Champaign, Illinois
dormitory lounge.

Rock Hudson singing to Doris Day,
...beautiful girl,
your eyes, your hair
is beyond compare...
(Pillow Talk)

"Touch me, touch me,"
guiding his hand
into her pleated wool skirt,
'petting' it was called,
one foot touching the floor at all times
ejaculating
somewhere or other
somehow or other
discreetly as possible
love in the 1950s.

He sees giant mushroom cloud
father of the H-Bomb Edward Teller

an entire island,
Eniwetok,
radioactive coral dust
a gigantic cauliflower, blue and gray
and mauve...
five million tons of TNT

Police Action Korea Harry Truman
and Dwight David Eisenhower,
each with six legs and arms
dancing to the music
of Lord Shiva and Judy Garland,
John, George, Ringo and Paul,
Lennon, McCartney, Harrison and Starr

doing it
on a pink velvet loveseat

some twenty-five miles into the stratosphere,
and spread a hundred miles across the sky.

Where Were You When?

Colin Morton

When I was just fourteen and
played on the team first string
I was horny as hornets and JFK
was my ideal (I admit it now)

but hey – "He was my brother"
who fell that autumn during playoffs
put graveyards not goalposts on the front page

and though I wandered out hotter than ever after
I half-knew I'd get no satisfaction on those icy streets
a half-step short of the sad end of love.

Now in DC decades later I visit
not Arlington but the wall, sunken tombstone
of space age innocence, brothers and sisters
who lay down for the echo of a memory of a lie

for the hero who is always too human to rule
for the peace these pilgrims carry away in their tears
for what balm they may deliver.

Discovering Desire

Ronnie R. Brown

That winter everyone was so sad. Even the holidays couldn't erase the image of little John—John Kennedy saluting his daddy's funeral procession. So, when someone suggested a party to watch the Beatles on Ed Sullivan, even though it *was* on a Sunday night parents relented.

It started around five, music, dancing. Just seventeen she was different–artsy, literary and very, very poor. Still, this time even she was invited to the big house with the big T.V.

Long before Ed Sullivan said "Ladies and Gentlemen, the Beatles!" some guy had sidled over. And when they sang "*"She loves you...*" he looked into her eyes and sang "yeah," nodded for her to say "yeah" and then the whole room joined the lads from Liverpool, shouting "YEAH!"

That was when he kissed her. Oh she'd been kissed before—sloppy dive-bomb kisses from boys at the Youth Dances, saliva—soaked kisses from a pimple-faced lifeguard at the lake—but this was different. Electricity shot through her body as their tongues danced to the Beatles and she felt honest-to-god desire for the very first time.

Of course, he had a girlfriend and when she saw them walking hand-in-hand the next week at school he looked right through her. But, to this very day, whenever she hears the Beatles some—thing inside her shouts "Yeah!" and for the length of the song she feels what it is to be truly alive.

As of early evening, Sunday, February 9, 1964, I still had not heard a single word about the Beatles. Somehow, in my isolation, I had not experienced a solitary note of their music, nor had I read a jot or tittle concerning their impending appearance on The Ed Sullivan Show. My bachelor uncle, who lived with us in our house on the farm, knocked on my bedroom door, advising me, "You had better come downstairs and see this"—meaning—something special was about to occur, something momentous, something I must see. Reluctantly, I joined my mother, father, sister, and uncle in the parlour for the viewing. Ed Sullivan, the neckless, gormless, slick-haired announcer who had already inflicted the weird mouse puppet Topo Gigio on an unappreciative generation of children, came on stage to introduce "these youngsters from Liverpool ... The Beatles." I did not know that my life was about to change, as with the opening strains of "All My Loving" sung by left-handed bass guitarist Paul McCartney, I woke up!

That very moment on that very evening, I made up my mind to become left-handed. The following morning I ate my breakfast with a left-handed spoon. At school, I took up my fountain pen in envy of my sinister classmates Murray Bratt and Rick McKekran. I'd taken to wearing my watch on my right wrist and gripping my stylograph so the nib blotted the page like the slow and steady drip of blood from a pricked finger, I commenced the careful study of left-handed cursive. I copied notes from the board like a poor learner. The rest of the term, I slowed myself down with the shaky cursive of a nervous schoolboy. Like everyone else, I saw myself practicing to be in an English rock band. And I would be Paul. I would be the cute one, my left hand waving at the screaming crowd of pixilated girls.

John B. Lee

Third Trimester

Andreas Gripp

The Beatles are on Sullivan
and I'm about to be born.
There is no correlation
other than my mother
is watching them on television,

and though my eyes are developed
by now, they're closed inside her womb
but I swear I'm hearing something
with these new ears of mine
that I've never heard before
(not only this thing called "music"
but the frenzied screams of manic
American girls);

and yes, once I've entered the world,
the melodies meant for me will be
simple and patronizing,
designed to soothe,
make me slumber,
and I'll wail, scrunch my face
instead, demanding, in my own
wordless way, that the mobile
above my head somehow chime
She Loves You Yeah Yeah Yeah.

1964

Robert Cording

Outside my window, four palm trees
shake their mop-tops in the windy cold
like they're the Beatles, and it's 1964 . . .
and I'm fifteen, stretched out before the altar
of a console TV, the wooden doors opened
because it's Sunday, and television is allowed,
recompense for early morning attendance
at church. My father reads the paper,
something, no doubt, about JFK's assassination,
and perhaps the rumors of the war to come
in southeast Asia. My mother sews.
And just when I think Sullivan cannot speak
any more slowly, he lets out the magic words
"youngsters from Liverpool," and the audience explodes
and the night accelerates and the Beatles
"All My Loving" fills our living room,
and I'm looking at Paul looking at John,
and even they can't believe what is happening.

What is happening? — I've forgotten tomorrow
is Monday, forgotten the north Jersey sky
outside our door, and how, starless
and alien, it's always tinged with green
from a neighboring electric plant;
I've forgotten the tedious blocks
of 50 x 100 lots, and the ranch houses
with four basic floor plans we all live in.
The Beatles are in our living room,
and whatever is happening includes me
when Paul smiles his isn't-this-cool,
isn't-this-nuts smile. I'm shaking
my head, trying to make my too short hair

spill around my face, and I'm beginning
to think the world I know isn't the only one.

And when the Beatles go right into
"She Loves You," I'm all *Yeah, Yeah, Yeah,*
so far outside my usual self
I let my father's complaints about the lyrics
slip by uncommented on. And even now,
forty years later, I can see their smiling faces.
We're all there in the living room,
my mother humming along, my father
lost behind the Sunday papers, and me,
unimaginably free, shaking myself alive,
summoned into a future knowing so little
and wanting so much, armed with
nothing more than joy and wonder.

You should be glad

Roger Bell

When first I hear that Beatles' song on the radio, I am instantly ecstatic, whirling around the bedroom. It's a "gotta have". I thump downstairs, leap on my bike and pedal furiously up to Ernie's drug store, which is kitty corner to the other drugstore, run by Jack. My mom buys drugs from Jack; she used to work in that store when she was younger and it was run by Luckhams; she is therefore fiercely loyal to it. When I was small I would go in just to watch Jack grind things with his mortar and pestle. My fascination now lies at Ernie's, where I buy my records. If he doesn't have what you want, he orders it in for you.

Directly inside the front door are bins filled with the latest 45s, each nestling inside its paper cover so that you can pick it up and check out the label. There is the red of RCA Victor with the dog stuffing his head into the gramophone, the more austere blue and silver of Philips and of London, the black and silver of Chess, the gold of Parkway and REO, the burgundy of Apex, the sunbright yellow with the word EPIC inside a black oval sunburst, and the circus rainbow of Decca. But what I am looking for that day is the spirals of orange and yellow that signal Capitol. When you have those records on the turntable and look down at them the colours swirl seductively.

"Do you have "She Loves You"?" I breathlessly ask Ernie. "Do we?" he demands of his daughter, who is working in the back. When she comes up front and searches through the bins, my knees grow weak. She's a year ahead of me in school, very smart, very cute. Green-eyed and freckled. I grow faint around girls like that. In fact, I grow faint around *all* girls right now. I am looking at the pale white backs of her knees below the hem of her plaid skirt. She turns, smiles at me and for a minute I forget why I'm there until I see the paper sleeve she's holding out to me. "Our only copy," she says. "You're the first in town to have it. " And she smiles again at me so hard every hormonal pimple on my red face feels as if it might burst. Before that happens and adds to my humiliation, I mumble my thanks, take the record to Ernie, pay my dollar and race home again. Up the stairs, snap the little yellow hole spacer into the record, slide it over the spindle, let it drop, swing the tone arm over, hold my breath as it descends into place... and the Mop-Tops explode from the speaker.

All afternoon, over and over and over, I play "She Loves You". My father yells up the stairs that maybe I want to give it a break, play something else. I play the B side, "I'll Get You". I play it twice, lose interest, go back to A. Yeah yeah yeah. Infectious. Around and around spiral the orange and yellow. I love this music, almost all music, have ever since I was confined to a darkened bedroom for much of the summer with red measles and my main companion was CKLW in Windsor/Detroit, playing mostly country music during the day then rock at night. And, when the sun went down, distant rock stations like WXYZ in New York and WGR, the Goodwill Station in Chicago, became clear. The music is in me like some happy disease. I'm glad all over, just like the Dave Clark Five sing.

I'm in bits and pieces of ecstasy. I listen avidly in those precious moments before I have to get out of bed in the morning, after school out in the yard on our new Japanese transistor radio, at night while I wade through Latin and math. I tackle the chapter called "The Dress of a Roman Woman" (which the book's previous owner has cleverly altered to "The [Un]Dress[ing] of a Roman Woman") while Bobby Vee croons that "she wore blue velvet"; I imagine Ernie's daughter wearing blue velvet, then wearing nothing...and though there is no one there to see it, my face goes scarlet. And I can rip through parabolic equations with Jan and Dean not backing off on Dead Man's Curve. I read the word *subsumed* in a book recently. Music has subsumed me, and what a drowning it is.

My mother knocks on my door interrupting my umpteenth playing of the record. "Fred is downstairs for you." I descend to where Fred waits. He is tall and twitchy and has big hair. He wants to be a disc jockey in Toronto, and he is even more mad for music than I am. "Is it true?" he asks? "Is what true?" I know exactly what he means but I want to drag out his pain. I also read the word *schadenfreude* recently. "Is it true that you are the only one in town with "She Loves You"?" "Yep." "I gotta have it," he begs. I think he'd fall on his knees before me and wrap his long arms around my calves and kiss my feet if my parents weren't here. "I'll give you five bucks for it." Is he nuts? I hesitate. "I just bought it, Fred." "Okay, then..." he licks his lips, "ten bucks," and he whips a tenner out of his pocket, proffers it. God, he really *does* need it.

"My mom interrupts, "But Fred, you can just..." I cut her off by snatching his money and saying, "Follow me."I know what she is going to say, he can just go up to the drugstore and order it and have it in two days. But he needs it now and I need to profit from his mania. We get to my room, and when he looks at the turntable his face nearly splits with the grin. "One last time, then it's all yours." He nods, too overcome to speak. I play it, we both sing along. It ends, I slide it off the spindle and into its sleeve, hand it to him, ceremoniously. No kidding, he is trembling so much he can barely hold onto it. I am too as I fondle the ten in my pocket. "Now you are the only one in town with "She Loves You"," I say as I herd him down the stairs and out the front door. As soon as he's turned the corner, I am on my way back up to the drugstore. Ernie's daughter is behind the counter. She smiles, but I do not falter this time, I am on a mission. "I'd like to order a copy of "She Loves You"," I say. She looks quizzically at me, I slap down the ten dollar bill, "and", I add emphatically, the great wheeler dealer of all time, "I want "Wipeout" by the Surfaris and "I Get Around" by the Beach Boys and "Surf City" by Jan and Dean and "It's Judy's Turn to Cry" by Leslie Gore and "It's Over" by Roy Orbison... "Will you slow down?" she said, "I can't write that fast." I add, more slowly, four more discs. "They'll be here in two days," she says.

And they are. My collection of 45s has just doubled. Yeah yeah yeah mixes with the percussive insistence of *Wipeout* and Roy Orbison's strings-backed breakup tears and the surf-sweet harmonies of the Beach Boys. For two days Fred has been happy, the only one in town.... "It was worth the ten bucks," he says to me after I tell him he is no longer special, and he isn't just trying to justify his impulsiveness. It *was* worth it. Some things just are.

Let It Be Imperfect

Michael Schatte

There is a five-second event during the Beatles' second *Ed Sullivan Show* appearance in 1964 which, if not of critical importance to popular music history, is certainly of paramount import to this brief essay. Two minutes and forty seconds into their rendition of "This Boy", the grey-suited Liverpudlian lads engage in a musical joke which half a century later begs to be contrasted against the humourless and over-produced and frequently lip-synched televised live 'performances' of the modern era.

There's the cute Beatle Paul, launching into an unplanned and silly sounding falsetto harmony, his voice mimicking and, I would argue, mocking the predictably satisfying three chord resolution of the song's chorus. I call it unplanned because it clearly was. Upon hearing Paul's bit of playful, high-pitched vocalizing, John Lennon shoots a surprised and humoured look at his bandmate, visibly holding back laughter as his smile is answered by a knowing and mischievous McCartney grin. That little exchange, dear reader, is what I regard as a perfectly imperfect convergence of musicality and humanity. It is a moment of significant insignificance, if you'll forgive the additional contradictory wordplay, and it is representative of much that is missing from the perfection obsessed live and recorded musical productions we are expected to consume in the 21st century.

It is my contention that the biggest musical acts of the digital era[1] engage more in a low-level, choreographed form of musical theatre (I would rather say musical *circus*, in deference to the many fine thespians still active) than the kind of spontaneous musical performance practiced by the best acts of yore.[2] In this approach, raw emotion and ability are superseded by a forensic level of sonic manipulation on stage and in the studio, with a salad of negative results. The reasons for this sea-change in our musical culture are many, but the point consistently missed by the purveyors of contemporary music is that there remains a popular appetite for real talent performing honest, original music without the technological safety nets now relied upon by so many acts. The tightrope metaphor has been done to death but holds true: music, whether in the recording studio or live, is simply more compelling and exciting when artists perform on the precipice of mini-disaster, with only their skill to blame or praise as the situation demands. A bad note, a missed chord change, a 'pitchy' vocal, and the band plays on. Often these natural mistakes are far more acute in the mind of the performer than in that of the average listener, and given time they frequently come to be regarded as so-called happy accidents if the performance has been captured for later consideration (Lennon's feedback intro to "I Feel Fine", anyone?). But the happy accident cannot occur if it has been fixed *in provectus*, with the audience therefore deprived of the kind of enriching moment illustrated by the live Beatle example above.

In the recording studio as on stage, The Beatles set a high standard for perfect imperfection. Yes, their albums are smooth, and yes, they are heavily treated with such studio effects as compression, tape delay, and other forms of distortion. But these effects are rendered with taste, and with a clear goal to maintain and complement the original performances while enhancing the inherent musicality of the whole. The Beatles worked without the ability to digitally tune and time-alter their tracks, a capability artists and producers now abuse as if music was nothing but math and its rough edges fit for the sander lest listeners hurt themselves on a slightly jagged guitar riff. Granted, there were at least two musical geniuses in the Beatles, and most popular acts of the present day cannot claim a single one and might thus be seen to benefit from the computerized help. But from a purely technical standpoint none of the fab four were instrumental virtuosos. George Harrison's guitar playing, for example, improved dramatically between 1962 and 1970, and there is still an intriguing quality to his early hollow body electric guitar work despite its relative choppiness. In a modern studio environment, George would be asked to re-play those parts twelve times so that the best bits from six of those takes could be melded together to form one ideal take. The result would sound utterly forgettable in comparison to the rich – yet imperfect – Harrison guitar work we are left to enjoy to this day.

Should you wish for further examples of what I am describing, consider the following. A quick visit to YouTube, the world's free jukebox and the pleasant mask on the ugly face of online music piracy, yields several isolated Beatle tracks that should shame the many thousands of vocalists who have allowed their performances to be digitally 'tuned' in the decade since this technology became ubiquitous. In these illegally uploaded YouTube examples can be heard the soloed vocal tracks from the second side of *Abbey Road*, smuggled by some intrepid thief out of the studio presumably during the recent – and to these ears, triumphant – remastering of the entire Beatle catalogue. To listen to the voices of Lennon and McCartney without the accompanying instrumentation is to marvel at not only their incredible talent, but the beauty of their decidedly human undulations of pitch. I contend that if the Beatles were a young band recording today under the auspices of a typical major label recording contract, those and other imperfections would be 'corrected' as a matter of course, and the long-term impact of the music greatly degraded as a result. We consumers of music are better off for the flubbed McCartney bass note, the slightly off time Starkey drum fill, the Lennon voice-shredding during *Twist and Shout*, and the Harrison sitar squeak. We could certainly live without the song *Yellow Submarine* in its entirety, but the other mistakes are nothing short of precious.

As modern ears become conditioned to regard auto-tuned vocals and computer sequenced drum grooves as normal in both the live and recorded musical contexts, we risk losing the ability to rejoice in music that was actually performed as one hears it. I suspect that the only music that will be considered interesting and worthy of the attentions of a posterity besieged by media are those performances that have maintained this sense of the organic, this sense of the human. What catalogue could be more deserving of long-term cultural awareness than that of the Beatles? When incredible talent is allowed to blossom and produce the kind of vital music that emerged from eight sweet years of recorded Beatle output, we are reminded that a price will be paid for the plasticity, predictability, and digitized 'perfection' of so many modern recordings and live perform-ances. That price is the complete apathy of future listeners, and deservedly so. Speaking words of wisdom, let it be imperfect.

1 – Measured loosely by ticket sales, radio airplay, Youtube 'hits,' and their ability to invade my sphere of attention despite concerted efforts to avoid them.

2 – For an ongoing example of this old-world performing craft, consider any Bob Dylan concert past, present, or future. The artist formerly known as Zimmerman holds to a naturalistic performance philosophy still, even as a portion of fans leave his concerts underwhelmed by the conspicuous lack of on-stage pyrotechnics literal and figurative, to say nothing of a voice that grows gloriously more ragged by the year. The editor of the present volume can attest to a similar live performance commitment from Paul McCartney (though with a far more elaborate production value than Dylan), despite how easy it would be for the former Beatle to simply let the computers run the show and continuing collecting his ample compensation after each appearance.

One, Two, Three, Foourrraah ....

Robert Hilles

A month after the Beatles played the Ed Sullivan Show for the first time our house burned down and we lost everything. We moved to a two-room shack a mile farther east from town. We lived there the rest of 1964, the year when Beatles songs played constantly on the radio. I'd lie on my bed at night and press the twelve-transistor radio to my ear and listen to WLS from Chicago, a station I found by travelling the dial late at night.

A week after the fire my father took my brother, sister and me to see what was left of the house. It had snowed in the interim so the ashes lay beneath pillowy clumps of white. The snow was unevenly spread about the ruin and some relics were still visible while others I had to brush aside snow to see properly: An incomplete set of bones near the front door (our dog had perished in the fire), the tangled legs of our Arborite table and chairs, the melted springs and frame of my parent's bed, and within that, the burnt core of the Knit King 4500 knitting machine a travelling salesman convinced my mother to buy the prior year. She never got the proper hang of it and put it under their bed for later. The control knob misshapen and blackened by the fire lay exposed and next to it the metal track she slid it along melted to a fist-sized lump. I dug that out of the snow and tossed it into the trees.

Standing amongst the snow and ruin that March 1964, the anaemic sun between stern clouds, I realized that abrupt change comes most often in the dead of winter when the intense cold normally slows everything to a standstill. That winter, Beatles music and the fire, and its terrible aftermath, triggered the impulse to write—polarities a necessity of art. I wrote lyrics at first and later poems.

In 1964 I didn't have a record player nor did most of my friends. A few of the affluent kids had a hi-fi in their homes. In early June of

1964, I went to Derek S.'s house after school one afternoon and listened to the Beatles album *Long Tall Sally* on his parent's RCA hi-fi. He'd bought the album the week before at Strain's Stationary. I'd perused record albums there a few times, but they were always sealed. Derek showed me how to open it and slide out the record from its sleeve and place it on the turntable and drop the needle on a song. I liked that we could play the songs in any order we liked and as often as we liked and not have to wait for a disc jockey to play them. That afternoon we repeatedly listened to the first two songs on Side A: *I Want to Hold Your Hand,* and *I Saw Her Standing There.* They filled the room in ways music hadn't done before. I could hear each instrument more clearly and other sounds too like handclapping and Paul's enthused count off: *one, two, three, foourrraah*.... that flowed right into the song.

That winter my childhood ended in the ruin of our house, leaving much unfinished. Until then my life had been a slow waltz but it sped up after that keeping pace to those up-tempo songs that ended exactly where they should, nothing missing.

Simple chords, drum beats, and harmonies created out of imperfection but forming perfect musical moments. Each song jazzed with intense, youthful intent, playful and earnest, exuding raw potential. Whenever I listen to *I Saw Her Standing There* and its iconic opening and then that fast, infectious beat and sparkling vocals, I hear that whole crazy year squeezed into just under three minutes.

Michael J. Wilson

then i got jealous— my sister's teeny-bop lust for hairy Beatles

a bagpipe playing somewhere down the block... inside, mom and the Beatles

the danciest girls, girls dancing with girls, dancing to those darn Beatles

my all white album, experiment stuffed ...and two faint beer-bottle stains

I've loved the Beatles from the time I heard the very first note of their performance on Ed Sullivan, but as a twelve-year old boy I had little or no opportunity to buy their records isolated as I was in a remote farm-house locked deep in southwestern Ontario. My mother noticed my enthusiasm for the band and being a kind and loving woman, she found and purchased the album Beatle Mania recorded by a knockoff band called the Schoolboys. She didn't know the difference. The sleeve was a shocking nail-polish pink with a crude black-ink drawing of five (not four) longhaired pretenders looking just enough like the fab four to fool her. She proudly presented her grocery-store gift to her disappointed son. Without a word of thanks, I took the LP to my bedroom, ripped open the plastic seal, pulled the vinyl from the sleeve and ran the sharp point of my pencil-box compass over the surface, thereby murdering the possibility of sound deep in the groove. After I'd vandalized the shiny black surface of the record with a disgruntled scrimshaw, I proceeded to deface the entire sleeve, scrawling—these are not the Beatles!!!—over and over again, the chemical stink of the marker blackening the fuchsia cardboard. Soon enough, I found myself shuffling through the record bin at the town pharmacy, with money in my pocket, and thus I managed to purchase my own copy of the bona fide Beatlemania, by the lads from Liverpool, the genuine article, John, Paul, George and Ringo. I never told my mother what I'd done with her gift. I'm slightly ashamed, but then they weren't the Beatles. No one else was.

As for my wife, she tells me that when she was a young girl her father bought her a copy of Long Tall Sally. And to this day she has no idea when or where he acquired it, or how he knew it was exactly what she wanted.

John B. Lee

Now We Lived

Ron Smith

O, Jaul, Pohn, Reorge, and Gingo! O,
global cynosures! O how you rolled
American rock! So selfmainlytaught, skiffle-
sniffing, so(on) —discarding, you
quarried y(our) surging obsessions, y(our)
one-night brands till Parlophone parlayed you
into her— and himicanes of marrowpounding.
                                                                                    You
pleased pleased us in ways we never knew
we pleaded needing, pulled our parents' cars
onto shoulders, clamped our skulls
with freakish phones, Beatlesplodingmania
detonating like a president's brains, everything
different, everything coming apart, everything
coming together . . .
                                        Now we lived
bugeared lives of quiet frenzy, fuzzy
with the tingling time, something
was up, something fizzing
like toniced gin, finding
us, fingering all our secret foldings,
a thousand twangling instruments, carnivals
of streamingsteamorganthinkingness,
ludiclabiallyrics lowlaughing, then
rising, highrising to historic hysterias . . .
                                                                            O, you
were the boys for bullet-riddled bulletins,
for lurching America growling into the jungle,
killing its kings, its kennedys, jamming
warm guns into womanly hands. All was
unhedonhbitedism, all experitimothylear-
itation

outside my closed dorm door, where I,
mured up in a wall of wishdom, strapped myself
down with pigmuscle . . .

In my personal dark I
peppered my rubbed-raw heart with GeorgeJohn's Dali-
drippings . . . What did I think was happening?
Gameday was my hallucinogen and Livesay's plaster
wall we stayed up all night ruining with spiral
galaxies, black-light bottomlessnesses . . .
the Beatles
retreated into their genius. Who could blame them?
Out of their apple wormed our sinvation, chaos
choruses of our harmodissonance, a new
nihil-hope-ism . . . The boys (still) plucked
little berries, toppled fat dominoes, puffed
smoke rings round the hollies, kracked
and konjured the bloody klassical . . .
while I
knocked people down, limped to class,
iced purple ankles, boiled my body, Platoed
my Emerson, Byornized my Bertrand Russell . . .
The stars, the stars were falling . . .

1970: the Boys disbeatled. We groaned, some of us
howled. The decade shuddered on, reeking
of napalm. We slogged, cynical, sick.
1980: A man with my college roommate's name
shot down Lennon for as good a reason
as most. O, my son, I want to hold your
strawberry fields forever. You are always
eleven, always wide-eyed on the side

of your narrow bed, looking
at my mouth.
                              And George, too,
is only a sound now the wind makes
keening through me. Paul
doriandroops on our TVs.
                                                    Ringo, O
goofy neglected one, are you locked up
behind a moat warding off cancer with wands
and vitamins? When you go out, do you go
in skinhead disguise and beatleproof vest?
When you traverse the river with your
crossed sticks and stretched skins, will you
cruise the surface or bubble below in the
pressurized *κίτρινος* you will own at least as long
as Wordsworth the daffodils?

Squash Heels

Julie Berry

black and white squash heels with pointed toes
and where the black patent leather
met the white
    —snap-on checkered bows

bought for my first day of high school
broken in at Maple Leaf Gardens where live
the Beatles second Toronto concert took place
in the year of our Lords 1965
the shoes lifted me an inch, maybe two
providing a slightly elevated view
it wasn't so much the added height
but the chic of the shoe

high in the grays at the Gardens
ceiling close enough to touch
I wanted to scream, I did
prayed to cry or even pass out
but it just seemed silly to do it
in squash heels
black and white squash heels with pointed toes
and where the black patent leather
met the white
    —snap-on checkered bows

The Beatles at Maple Leaf Gardens

~ Toronto, Ontario, September 7, 1964

I.B. Iskov

It did not matter
what they performed
in matching grey suits
like businessmen
negotiating notes
in the din of thousands
of crazy-in-love-teenage-girls.

I didn't want that night to end.
The thrill of John, Paul and George
bending back and forth,
strumming guitars
with Ringo in the background,
long hair swaying from side to side,
briskly banging the drums
to the back-beat of my heart.

My childhood ended then and there.

Suffering pangs of unrequited love
like an ignored wallflower,
I cried my fourteen-year-old eyes out
wishing it was my hand they wanted to hold
knowing I would never, ever, ever
get to meet them.

John, Paul, George, Gary and Ringo ... Or How I Spent My Summer Vacation on August 17, 1966

Gary Schatte

* BORN, June 21, 1951, Ontario, Canada.

* BORN AGAIN, November 1963. Hear THE BEATLES for the first time.

* BORN AGAIN, AGAIN, Wednesday, August 17, 1966. See THE BEATLES live at Maple Leaf Gardens, Toronto, Ontario.

<u>Meet the Beatles – One Sunday Evening, November 1963</u>

Darkness outside my bedroom. Music emanating from the gray plastic six inch cube of a radio on my night table. The announcer declares...

"Here's a great new band from England playing '*Please Mr. Postman*'... the Beetles."

[This should be interesting. I love Please Mr. Postman by the Marvelettes.]

"D-liver, D-letter, D-sooner, D-better..."

[O MY GOD. HOW IS IT POSSIBLE THAT THIS BAND COULD MAKE THIS SONG SO MUCH BETTER, SO MUCH MORE EXCITING, THAN THE ORIGINAL? THIS GROUP IS INCREDIBLE!]

"Wait a minute. Wait a minute. Oh yeah. You gotta wait a minute, wait a minute, oh yeah... Check it and see, one more time for me."

Hair raising. Only band that made every cover better than the original. You really got a hold on me J,P,G and R. Did anybody ever make a Beatles song sound better than the original? OK, maybe Cocker – sorry Ringo.

Ed Sullivan – February 1964.

Enough said.

Breathless Anticipation – 1964 to 1966

Can't wait for each new Beatles album. Never disappointing, ever evolving. Feels like I'm growing right along with them. Wear out the needle, wear out the record, wear out my ears.

Nine albums released by Capital Records Canada up to and including Rubber Soul. RIPPED OFF BY CAPITAL: only 11 songs on each album while the Brits get 14 (a mere 6 songs on each soundtrack album!).

The Contest – FIRST PRIZE – August 1966

Capital Records Canada 1966 Contest.

"D-liver, D-letter...". Opened our mailbox, August 10, 1966...

"Dear Gary:
We are pleased to inform you, you have won our first prize of two 2 tickets to 'The Beatles Concert' at Maple Leaf Gardens at 8:30 p.m. on August 17th, 1966."

TWO 'FLOOR' TICKETS ENCLOSED.

PEEL ME OFF THE CEILING...PLEASE!!!

August 17th, 1966

Mom's birthday. THE BEATLES TONIGHT. 2 hours drive from London, Ontario. Must leave on time.

7:00 p.m. Summer warmth, scalpers outside, sidewalk vendors, hot dog smells, the famous Maple Leaf Gardens. No hockey game was ever this important. Sorry Foster.

THE SHOW

ON THE FLOOR ... HALF WAY BACK. Constant buzz of mostly female voices. 'Beatles 65' playing over the sound system. I feel fine.

Lights go down. Flash bulbs popping. Unbelievable atmosphere.

Why so many opening acts??...

THE REMAINS. (When are THEY coming out?)

BOBBY HEBB. (When the hell are THEY coming out?)

THE CIRCLE. ('Red Rubber Ball'. SHIT. WHEN ARE THEY COMING OUT??!!)

THE RONETTES (OK. This MUST be the last warm up act.)

M.C. Hits the Stage:

"LADIES AND GENTLEMEN...JOHN, PAUL, GEORGE AND RINGO... THE BEATLES!"

* SCREAMING. CRYING. STANDING ON SEATS. FAINTING. AMBULANCE ATTENDANTS.

"Just let me hear some of that Rock and Roll music..."

* MOVE UP FOR A CLOSER LOOK.

" (feedback) Baby says she's fine you know, she tells me all the time you
know..."

* CAN BARELY HEAR THE SONGS. JUST ENOUGH TO KNOW WHAT SONG IT IS. WHO CARES!!!

"I wanna be your lover baby..." (shake that head Ringo!)

* THIS MUST BE A DREAM.

"She's a big tease-ah..."

* 11 SONGS

"Turn me on when I get lonely..."

* 28 MINUTES

"Well I saw Uncle John with Long Tall Sally..."

* IT'S OVER.

POSTLUDE – After the Show. Sam the Record Man on Yonge St. is open late.

Pick up newly released Revolver album. Listen to it all the next day. "Turn off your mind relax and float down stream...".

INNOCENT NO MORE.

Scream

Betsy Struthers

Pleading, sulking, crying in the end get us almost what we want, tickets to the Beatles concert, but only in the afternoon and in the grays (*far from the crush,* Mom says) and on the condition that Sis and I stick together the whole time from the moment we get on the subway to the moment we get home. To be there, we will agree to anything. We nod our heads, we promise truce.

Such a crowd blocks Carleton Street in front of Maple Leaf Gardens and so many cops and what are all the ambulances for? We hold hands, we glare at anyone who presses too close (Mom hissing *pick-pockets, purse snatchers, fanny feelers*).

Long climb to the rafters to find our seats. Surrounded by girls, dazed by the size of the rink we have seen only on TV, its cold white covered with rows of chairs surrounded by staggered ranks of bleachers. Noise on the stage so tinny and weak beneath the surf of chatter, we don't listen to the other acts, we bicker over Dad's binoculars, who gets to use them first.

A collective gasp, held breath: they wander on, bent over their guitars, Ringo hops up behind his drums. *Well, shake it up, ba...* and the rest is drowned. Drowned as we fling ourselves, are flung as jetsam in the surge, on our feet, reaching out, clutching each other, binoculars forgotten, the tiny figures barely visible in the blizzard of notes and roses thrown at them. Gulping air, tears. Can't hear my own voice in the roar that envelopes me, lifts me above them all to float down the river of spotlight into John's arms – though I don't move, packed as I am between Sis and the girl next to me who has collapsed sobbing against my shoulder. *Help, I need somebody...*

When it's over, we slump in our seats as others shuffle past, limp, spent. Sis's face a mask of streaked mascara, smudged lipstick. She's panting softly now, eyes closed, hands folded on her breasts as if in prayer. My shift plastered to my spine, thighs gummed together, parched throat. Ears tingle in the aftermath. The scream that fades into this little death.

Note: I saved the ticket stub from the concert, have kept it in my wallet for years; it is now pictured on the back cover of this book.

I can only recall my father ever taking us to the movies on two separate occasions. We went to see 'Sink the Bismarck'. I suppose we went to see that movie because my father's brother had served in the Canadian Navy during World War Two, and although he had not been involved in that particular engagement, he had been a veteran of the D-Day invasion of Normandy. In the early morning hours of June 6, 1944, he was part of a crew stationed on a minesweeper charged with clearing the English Channel in the ominous darkness before the major assault on the beaches of France. The men had been called together and forewarned that they were not likely to survive the night. They were told to get their work done and get the hell out of the way before the Americans came or they would be blown out of the water by the Yanks. Dad insisted we see that black-and-white war film. I was nine years old, and it was February 1960. That evening as we headed for the theatre, I suffered an excruciating headache. I'd slipped on a patch of ice on the school ground during recess and cracked my head thereby losing the remainder of the day, having suffered a blackout that lasted for hours.

The only other occasion Dad ever took us to see a movie was when we viewed the rerelease of my mother's favourite film Gone with the Wind. It was playing in the mid nineteen sixties at the deluxe Fox Theatre located on Woodward Avenue in Detroit City. We were making our annual trek, cross-border shopping for school supplies and sundries when shoes and clothing were cheaper in America. As I recall, we sat in the movie-house darkness, and when Big Sam said, "I say when it's quittin' time," and then he'd bellowed "It's quittin' time ..." and a black lad rang the evening bell riding the bell wheel with his small body shadowed in the cotton-harvest light of a Georgia gloaming, at that exact moment, Dad stood up, walked out of the darkness into the plush lobby where he spent the remainder of the time until the movie was over sitting alone in the popcorn aroma of the crimson carpet foyer. Not wishing to waste his time frittering away a precious afternoon watching the grand sweep of Cecil B. Demille's elegy for the lost glory of the Confederacy in decline, he'd rather sit by himself in the fading glory of an old theatre gone to seed.

So, given my father's proclivity, I despaired of the opportunity to see A Hard Day's Night, the first Beatle film when it came to Chatham, a town located twenty impossible miles away from the home farm. Fortunately, by then, Mother had acquired her driver's license. She seemed to intuit how important it was for my sister and me to see that film. I was so grateful when the lights dimmed in the movie house, because someone had seen fit to slip the following caution tagged into the loop before the start of the film—"Absolutely no screaming allowed! We will stop the movie, and all screamers will be removed from the theatre—signed—the management."

As for my wife, she tells me that when she saw A Hard Day's Night in her hometown of London, Ontario, she couldn't hear a single word of dialogue or a single note of music for the relentless and hysterical screaming of the crowd.

I didn't get to see their second film Help at the theatre. The night it first aired on TV, I was lying on the floor in the farm parlour, as was my television viewing habit, in rapt attention, when cousin Ted and his parents George and Judy arrived for a visit. Ted joined me to watch the movie and his mother Judy inquired, "I didn't know you like the Beatles Johnny." To which my father rejoindered, "He doesn't." With that comment made, he snapped off the television set. Fortunately for me, cousin Ted protested and I got to watch most of the rest of the movie, until the coming in of foul weather stole the signal and the Beatles vanished into television snow.

John B. Lee

No, No, No

Amber Homeniuk

my father was mortified
that young girls
were allowed to carry on so
all the more reason
I held it in, silently
transported
while I didn't want it to stop
I wanted to hold
all of their hands
and that high note – *ooo*
so dangerous
those suits – no one had seen anything like it
and of course their hair
not a speck of Brylcreem
and how they shook it!
you did and you didn't know
so much about them
when they came to Toronto
I was dying a million deaths
to breathe the same air
they'd be so close
but there was no Ticketmaster
no one had credit cards
lucky ducks in the city
just hopped on the streetcar and went!
then on local radio
someone in town with two tickets
I called, they were mine
had the money
needed permission

he said
absolutely not, you are
not going to see those ginks
she said
you could be
trampled, lost, taken
and I had to call the lady back
the lights went out
I was forever missing out on so much
it's a wonder I didn't run away from home then

Lennon

Robert Priest

The sky was a blue throat with no scream
And then came Lennon raw with rage

There were no tears on earth
And Lennon was the salt and the rain

He bittered the air with his lament
And dared in the end utter hope

Then Lennon left
The songs blown from his chest

Beyond his soul
A split widening the sky

Where the world
Got bigger than the world

Could hold

He Loves Me Yeah, Yeah, Yeah Yeah

Susan Whelehan

John.

He was mine and I was his. All you had to do was open my 3-ring binder and read,"JOHN AND SUSIE FOREVER" printed in bubble letters of every colour all over the inside covers to know that. His pictures plastered my bedroom walls and he stared into my eyes from the Paladium poster taped to the ceiling above my bed. I had to baby-sit the Baker brats for an hour and a half to buy the 45 of "She Loves You" for 45 cents at Sears and when Sister Benedictus told me I had been a foolish, selfish, uncharitable child who should have put that money into the Mission box to ransom a pagan baby in Africa I knew I had to go to confession and would have to go to confession for the rest of my life because I was not going to stop buying Beatle records just so some pagan baby could be baptised and avoid the flames of Hell. I learned to live with the guilt by turning up the volume. "Well, shake it up Baby now..." John comforted my chubby Grade 6 self when he sang, "And I do appreciate you being 'round." He was singing just to me. Just to me. He was sooo handsome and funny and well, sexy and, okay, married but, never mind and when Pam and I read in Tiger Beat the date of his wedding and the date Julian was born we counted and realised they HAD to get married and we vowed we would never tell another soul, that it would be our secret. Well, and theirs. And it probably was until right now. So, don't tell another soul. And if regular Sunday mornings were Mass and the Holy Eucharist, The Body of Christ, then Sacred Sunday nights were The Ed Sullivan Show and the Beatles, the Body of John. I watched them on the TV in my parents' bedroom with the door closed so I could touch the screen and melt and whimper and afterwards I'd call Pam and we would scream together about every detail like "John sniffed!" "Paul winked!" "Did you see George do a little dance?" "Ringo ...well, was Ringo..." until my father yelled at me to stop screaming and hang up and I had to go and study for my Social

Studies test on Bolivia which I should have studied for before but couldn't because I was too excited about seeing him and couldn't after because I was too excited about having seen him and I was never going to go to Bolivia anyway but I was going to be his FOREVER.
And I am.

I Never Saw Them

On the 4th of June 1964, the inaugural concert of the Beatles' first world tour took place in Copenhagen. They never returned to that city.

Birgit Elston

I kiss both Paul and John goodnight
on their poster-mouths, and maybe
George,   and Ringo, who I never love
as much

but do I ever love those boots, with the heels
that all the boys wear
          they want to be rock stars, practice
with electric guitars every day after school
in their parents' garages
          we turn up to perform
Englishness
in mini-skirts, and platform shoes
and Union Jack carrier-bags slung casually
over the arm
as if just back from Carnegie Street

and Please, Please Me
and four boys from Liverpool, ready to soar
from the cover of their first LP, an everyday
occurrence
          if we were in Soho, or in Chelsey
not here
in suburban Lyngby, fretting about chemistry
lessons and math tests, calculating
the unlikely odds
of getting to the Beatles' concert in Copenhagen

—not a chance, my dad says
he has heard about love-crazed girls causing
havoc, screaming, fainting,
breaking the seats
        and so I must miss the biggest event
in a thousand years
and rock music is not allowed at our house
but I get Radio Luxembourg on my sister's
transistor radio, under the covers, in the dark
the dial glows like a sun
in my eiderdown cave, the Fab Four play
hide-and-seek
with parents, and teachers, and anyone
who cannot see
black-and-white turning to glorious colour.

        They are singing "This Boy",   I hear John
above the others
        an almost indiscernible break in his voice
reveals a softness that makes me want to cry. I dream
of going down the King's Road
hooking a finger under a longhaired boy's wayward
curl
and placing it softly behind his ear.

basement band

an excerpt from 'show of hands'

Laurie Smith

Kathy and Becky,
the two girls who had
white go-go boots,
DECLARED themselves
our band's
lead singers.
I felt this was not fair
since I was the only one
who knew all the words to
She Loves You.

It's You She's Thinking Of

Sandra Lloyd

She learned to play trumpet at summer school.
After years of piano, saxophone, clarinet, flute,
she surrendered finger play, the buzz of moist reeds,
lips pursed as if blowing across the mouth of a bottle
without a message.

With trumpet, a new set of facial muscles awoke. Her mouth
bruised and swollen, she worried this would hinder
kisses with a certain boy. She didn't want
her lips to be that sore.
She couldn't stand the pain.

She played "Here, There and Everywhere" that summer,
learned from words and a tender hook, the possibility
that a boy might desire closeness, might use her
to ease his worries. Concepts so simple
they seemed honest.

She played trumpet to offset restlessness, looked ahead
to autumn's renewal, to be near the boy who, it turned out,
would keep her waiting. Ultimately she gave up
on the boy (and the trumpet)
because she couldn't stand the pain.

Older, she's learning to play guitar, knows
that fingertips must endure an ache no one else will see
for the sake of patterns, progressions.
This demands her entire body,
not just mouth, tongue, lungs. As her guitar gently weeps
she's able to see the love there that's sleeping,
the lips she was missing.

Peachy

... everything gonna be all right, baby
Wolfman Jack gonna rock the night
the Wolfman, he understand
owROOOOOOooo

Amber Homeniuk

In '64 we were juice-heavy, grade nine girls
tight against the branch of home
as latched-on lips
dressed like our mothers
who never let us out un-girdled
because we'd jiggle, which invited
you know
flesh

anyway, we started looking to England
for everything, though our back-combed beehives
– underpinnings, net, floral fog of spray –
stayed hard
while the world
crumbled

I remember ruddy cheeks, pollen-cake lashes, fresh
velvet down skin, and being joined at the hip
to my transistor radio, it was a perfect coral-pink
the exact grooves of its bright gold dial
fit my calloused thumb
teething marks
imprinted

my tongue poked in the speaker holes
pressed past plastic to wire mesh, just
for the puffs of John's harmonica
bare breath of life
my lips inched along sharp seams
I licked electric vibrations
music dripping liquid, drool
this was for me, nectar
those four mop-tops
were for
me

still the mundane
would not be shivered loose
clung like garlic peel to wet fingers
every Saturday's brown spice cake
with white sugar icing
floor washed and waxed
on our knees
fried chicken Sunday
and fetch Freddie a fork
ear to the party line
perched on the wood box
one eye to Lassie
Wonderful World of Disney
and good old
Ed

a growing-up season, viewed
through the funhouse prism of TV news:
people out there were angry
all the racial unrest, how could we ever
understand what was happening?
an end to feeling safe, broken boughs
and vows, a drying peach stem
rocked free of its green bezel, black
fallen away, a dropped
umbilical
stump

the world was a whole new revolving thing
while here it all stayed put
roots in drab reality, same flat fields outside
and fresh-ironed shirts hung 'round the kitchen
dismal light through cotton
starched albatross wings
I was distracted by fashion, dreams, 16 Magazine
desperate for bright colour, heat
but left tasting silence
at the back of my mouth
I tried to protest once and still
had to fetch
the g.d.
fork

dust blown from shoulders
of a murky jar, peach preserves
bruised and brown, blood tang
feeling-rush back to my rusty fingers, tongue
syrup-sweet and keen as disappointment
the ripest expectations
turned against my teeth
to gouge
like a
clingstone
pit

The first time I heard "A Day in the Life," it was being broadcast on CFCO out of Chatham and I was listening to it on the truck radio accompanying my bachelor uncle to the local dump. Tragically, we arrived at our destination before the song was finished. Uncle John left the key in the truck ignition saying, "You sit there and listen to that." How he knew I needed that music almost more than oxygen was beyond my comprehension. I know for certain that my father would have killed the engine and insisted we get to work. He might even have added, "You don't like that," making it a statement of fact, though my soul might have cried out otherwise.

When I acquired a copy of Sgt. Pepper, and was playing it for one of my female cousins the first time she heard it, she inquired, "Do you really like that?" She'd been something of an early Beatle fan herself, but the tone of her inquiry gave the strong impression that the new Beatle record wasn't exactly to her taste. The Beatles had grown moustaches and were no longer the loveable teen idol moptops. Now they were young men. They'd left the bubblegum set behind, but the shiver in my spine and the tingle in my scalp confirmed that I too was evolving along with the music. I'd become too cool for the Monkees, and I was fixing a hole where the rain gets in that stops my mind from wondering where it will go ...

John B. Lee

Hey Jude

Richard M. Grove (Tai)

The last school desk chattered as it skidded across the black and white checkered floor, jammed up against the wall. The floor was swiped clean with the extra wide janitor push mop. Light fell in around the green pull blind on the classroom door. The teacher's desk lamp spilled an amber haze across the room. The mood was set.

It was the girls' choice dance. It was like a starter pistol echoed through the room, off the smudged blackboards, shimmering the drawn blinds closing off the bright afternoon light from the playground. All of the wallflowers scrambled for their target. Maria, from the other class, one grade older, strode at me like I was the only ice-cold pop left in the fridge and boy was she thirsty. Young love, how wonderful. How lucky could an adolescent boy be to have a girl just a bit taller than you with an ample bosom grab you close and press your peach fuzz face into her soft warm cleavage? Maria was my first big bosomed slow dance and boy did she know how to sway.

Hey Jude, don't make it bad.
Take a sad song and make it better.
Remember to let her into your heart,
Then you can start to make it better.

The year was 1968 and I was in grade 8. "Hey Jude" had been released only two or three months earlier. Everyone was in love with Paul McCartney's slow moving, almost sexy ballad. Everyone was in love with the Beatles. No one cared that it was supposed to have been written to comfort John Lennon's son, Julian, during "the" rock and roll breakup of the year.

Hey jude, don't be afraid.
You were made to go out and get her.
The minute you let her under your skin,
Then you begin to make it better.

"Ricky, dance!" were her only words. I didn't know if it was a drill sergeant command that I should salute to or a question that had no intended answer. I stood there in a crisp, high collared pale blue shirt, white socks showing from under my grey, flannel pants. I didn't say a word. "Hey Jude" whispered over the room.

And anytime you feel the pain, hey jude, refrain,
Don't carry the world upon your shoulders.
For well you know that it's a fool who plays it cool
By making his world a little colder.

Taunted by her bra strap my hands clenched her back as she pulled me in. Slowly my hands slipped to her waist. The four minute coda was the warmest ending to a song ever recorded. I had melted into a lump of malleable clay.

Hey jude, don't let me down.
You have found her, now go and get her.
Remember to let her into your heart,
Then you can start to make it better.

With sweating palms Maria and I stepped back and forth, swaying back and forth, back and forth. Swaying to the lyrics.

So let it out and let it in, hey jude, begin,
You're waiting for someone to perform with.
And don't you know that it's just you, hey jude, you'll do,
The movement you need is on your shoulder.

Maria was my first love. The affair lasted only as long as that 7 minute song. I can't say that I ever spoke to her again. She stood, hands clenched in front of her, wishfully, for the next 45 minutes while I goofed around with my buddies throwing baseball cards into the corner. Whoever's card stood the tallest won the round. My friends? I don't know who they were now, after all these years, but I remember Maria and her swaying with me for the eternity of "Hey Jude".

Hey jude, don't make it bad.
Take a sad song and make it better.
Remember to let her under your skin,
Then you'll begin to make it
Better better better better better better, oh.

Na na na na na ,na na na, hey jude...

Note: The Beatles' song "Hey Jude" was released in August 1968 as the first single from record label, Apple Records. More than seven minutes in length, "Hey Jude" was, at the time, the longest single ever to top the British charts. It also spent nine weeks at number one in the United States—the longest run at the top of the American charts for a Beatles single—and tied the record for longest stay at number one (until the record was broken by Debby Boone's "You Light Up My Life"). The single has sold approximately eight million copies and is frequently included on professional critics' lists of the best songs of all time.

I remember listening to Hey Jude/Revolution every night over the summer of 1968. It was a two-sided number one hit staying at number one for nine weeks straight. CFCO in Chatham played it every night around ten p.m.. I used to listen to a cream-white radio with a cheesy speaker. They'd play Hey Jude back to back with Revolution. I loved that fuzz guitar intro on Revolution. I loved McCartney's voice on Hey Jude. Every time I hear it I'm reminded of those torpid summer nights falling asleep in the heat of my farmhouse bedroom.

John B. Lee

Beatlemania, Ed Sullivan, Me and History

Honey Novick

"Yeah, Yeah, Yeah", they came to North America.

"Please, Please Me", they requested but I couldn't.

They, the Beatles, were ushered onto a stage already built,
brick by fantastic brick from the illusions and desires of
teenaged girls, me being the most 'fan'atic.
The theatre of my imagination was set.
Plank by plank, bit by bit, it was created by images cast of
swarthy, sweet, come-hither, up-turned-lip snarl of the forbidden.
These clean, cute guys from Britain were not it.

When I was 4 or 5 years of age, there was a "Mothers and Babes" summer camp north of Toronto. I was enthralled by the older kids who fished for catfish and listened to this new singer called "Elvis". My mother would ridicule him by singing "I'm All Shook Up" in a derisive Yiddish "Moishe Ba-kucked". Well, spur me on mother. However, her friend Dinah said, "listen to him, he's operatic". That bit of respect changed everything.

Later I became a fan of Pat Boone when I heard him sing "Love Letters in the Sand"

Then came the groundswell of pre-teen love – Ricky Nelson, Fabian, Frankie Avalon, Bobby Rydell. My room was papered with their teen idol magazine photos. I wrote to them and "they" wrote back, especially Ricky.
Don't call me on Wed. evening, I wouldn't answer when
"The Ozzie and Harriet Show, featuring Ricky Nelson" was on TV.
I bought paraphernalia, like photo albums and autograph books and pencil holders.
I was FAN Numero UNO, the frenzied prepubescent fan.

In time I knew something was missing and something needed to be said, but didn't know what and couldn't know how.

I did know "it", a sound, an energy, a spark. It trickled in from Buffalo, New York. snuck in from New York City and poured in from Detroit, Michigan, the Motor City, Motown. Music was coming in and I stood stalk still.
"Will You Still Love Me Tomorrow?" "I Met Him On a Sunday, Da Doo Ron, Ron", "Mama Said".
Chuck Berry already told us to "Roll Over Beethoven",
Little Richard was keening "Lucille" and "The Girl Can't Help It" and we couldn't ignore Jerry Lee Lewis pounding the piano with his feet.
TV was the new pop tool of a whole new popular world.

The girl groups opened the door for the boy groups, the Temptations, the Miracles.
This was YES, YES, OH YES, not Yeah, Yeah, Yeah.

I lived downtown. Our neighbourhood, and school were diverse.
We had afterschool dances.
I befriended, then gained the confidence and courage to ask one of the black boys
why he ironed his hair. He simply said, "to make it straight".
He also told me he put burning chemicals in his hair as well.

Was it hair that was turning into a major issue? Not yet.

And so with the Fabulous Fabian growling "Turn Me Loose", then reminding me he's a "Tiger", I didn't need any other heart throb.

I was twelve but could pass for 16 and often did,
like when I went to see but didn't understand "Peyton Place".

Slowly the sounds trickled in.
It wasn't just the Beatles that added to the cacophonic symphony of the early 1960's.
It was voices from Viet Nam.
It was the entitled voice of the USA government.
It was the hip and stylish voice of Jackie Kennedy.

It was the churring sounds of the night.
It was the voices of our neighbours who were no longer as open, especially those who ironed their hair.
There was a murmur, a buzz, a thrum in the air.
Could I hear it? Would I understand it?

One day my friend Dona and I were sitting on the porch stairs.
I said, "let's write a movie about us going to Hollywood and meeting movie stars".
(Believe it or not, it happened, not the movie, the trip).
Dona said, "let's go to Washington and march with Dr. King".
I had never heard of Dr. King up to that point.
Neither of us went physically, but we sure were there in spirit.
A whole new awareness opened for me.
A new kind of education was being taught.

By now I was 13 and in high school. Still a frenzied fan.
Elvis was drafted and had come home.
Bob Dylan broke through the ether to be heard, to enrage, to teach, to entertain, to inspire.
In the July 28/29, 1963 Newport Folk Festival, Dylan sang "Blowin' In the Wind" and became the Pied Piper Prince Regent of the new generation.
Unions, workers, Rimbaud, Blake, Dylan Thomas were subjects he carried in his guitar case.
"Don't Think Twice" was galvanizing and popularized by Peter, Paul and Mary.

Plank by plank the stage was transforming from this girl wanting to be entranced by the Philadelphia dark-haired, well-coifed Latin-lover beautiful boys to Motown group entertainers to Dylan shaking the rafters of my imagination and intellect.

Onto this stage the Beatles came. Yes, they were cute. So what? They didn't entice me.
Floating on the screeches of teen girls, catching the ears of Ed Sullivan and our parents, they entered our homes and pervaded our culture.
I could no longer ignore the invaders.
They brought style – bowl haircuts and collar-less jackets.

They were funny. You could actually dance to their music. Anybody who ever watched Dick Clark's "American Bandstand" knew that a song worked if you could dance to it. Just Listening to music was a new phenomenon.

Dylan and Joan Baez walked with Dr. Martin Luther King, Jr. on August 28, 1963.
Dr. King and his supporters actually organized the march to fight for better employment.
The march wasn't conceived of a civil rights issue until he spoke.
Who knew that it would be an iconic day in history?
Who knew that Dr. King would extemporize his "I Have A Dream peech"?
Dona and I didn't go but we were there.
"Non-violence" was just becoming a part of the lexicon of the day.
The Freedom Singers singing "This Little Light Of Mine" were formed to support voters' rights in the southern US.
Try as they might, the media could no longer turn a blind eye nor deaf ear to the voices, the thrumming of the cacophonic symphony.

87 days, exactly, after Dr. King spoke at the Washington Memorial, on Nov. 22, 1963, John F. Kennedy was shot and everything changed, FOREVER and FOR EVERYONE.

77 days after that on Feb. 9, 1964, the Beatles appeared on the Ed Sullivan Show.
They were contracted for 3 Sundays in a row.
Now, no one could ignore them any longer, especially me.

That day was a family day, a Sunday.
We visited Uncle Julius in the hospital.
Julius was always robust, round.
The man that sat by the window in a robe
was skeletal.
I was so horrified that I became silent, mute.
My heart was seared by this memory.
My dealing with life and death issues was non-existent, up to that day.
I didn't want to see Julius like that again. I never did.

Then on to Uncle Percy's.
They had a larger television and EVERY family I knew watched the Ed Sullivan Show.

By the time the Beatles opened the show, I was ready to scream.
I wanted to scream for Julius.
I wanted to scream for change.
I wanted to scream for me.
I wanted to scream against injustice.
I wanted to scream and in time I did.

I screamed for release.
I screamed because I was loud and high-pitched and it felt good.
I screamed because I was a teenager in North America.
I screamed because I could and no one would be frightened.
I screamed and suffered the ridicule but it felt good and alive.
I screamed for what I felt but couldn't express in words.
I screamed and screamed and began to sing and began to write.
I screamed until I became me.
Until that actually happened, I began to pay attention to these 4 guys from Liverpool.
I didn't care that they were cool.
I cared that they made me dance.
I cared that they helped me make friends.
I cared that they really helped me have a deeper understanding of art.

By the time I acquiesced to the music of the Beatles, their Long Playing album "Beatlemania" caught my attention.
What a wonderful piece of art.
I treasure it to this day.
The 4 musicians' portraits were on the cover in black and white.
One could see only half of their faces.
The other half was blackened. This was the drama of art – contrast, organization, style, simplicity.
It was all very avant garde. It was also mature and thoughtful.
It made me stop to take a look, to think, to admire or not,
to listen, to critique, to buy and to cherish and finally to love.
I didn't love George, John, Paul or Ringo the way I did Ricky or Fabian or Frankie or Bobby.
I loved John, Paul, George and Ringo because they brought me to a new level.
As a young music student, I was being developed by the choices I made.
Listening to the Beatles' harmony gave my ear a flavour.

Yes, it was different than the Motown boy group harmonies but not by much.
After all, they too, were influenced by African American music and culture.

My best friend in high school was a beautiful gay boy.
He wore Beatles' style, no-collar clothing and he could dance.
When we danced together, especially to the Beatles, we made a statement.
The Beatles crooned to a wonderful adaptation of the Miracle's
"You Really Got a hold on Me",
Our bodies spoke those words. We had to hold onto one another.
We were leading secret lives.
My friend's sexuality and me protecting him.
People looked. They commented. Our personages meant something.

"She's Got the Devil in Her Heart" gave me a sexiness never before discovered in myself
(after all I was only 14 years old)

"Do You Want To Know A Secret?" allowed me to start a conversation.

"I Wanna Hold Your Hand", a thought, but a decision of "not yet".

North Americans were all reeling from the assassination of JFK.
Civil Rights marches were heating up.
Voters rights were a head-scratching topic.
People were changing. I was changing.
I was forming opinions, learning through process.
Things were getting fast and furious.
News items dominated each and every life.
Lyndon Baines Johnson was president of the USA.
Lester B. Pearson was the Canadian Prime Minister.
"Mike" as he familiarly liked to be called felt an
imperative desire to initiate a Canadian flag.
Beatlemania was swelling and opening doors
for a formidable British invasion
(as if we in Canada weren't familiar with all things British).
Was Beatlemania a release from the awareness of change,
a distraction from the seriousness of things to come?
Cassius Clay wasn't yet Mohammed Ali but still pretty.

Malcolm X was alive and making sure his talking points were heard.
Kitty Genovese was stabbed to death as her neighbours just looked on.
Jack Ruby, a Jewish mobster, was tried for the death of Lee Harvey Oswald.
Liz and Dick got married in Montreal, the first time.
Sidney Poitier won an Academy Award, the first black man to do so.
The Rolling Stones couldn't get "no satisfaction" and radio stations wouldn't play their "dirty" music.
At 14, I made my first political move.
I called the station and told them I want to hear this music because I, too, "ain't got no satisfaction" and the Stones were speaking for me.

And then things got focused, like a volcano getting ready to flow...
Aug 4, 1964 the bodies of Schwerner, Goodman and Chaney were found in Mississippi.
The Northern Boys went south, for a humanistic purpose.
The Southern Good Ole Boys killed them and left their bodies to rot.

And so change came to North America and the world.
I was an usher, opening the door to change,
lighting its way down the aisle of this theatre,
showing it to its seat
and making sure change was comfortable.

I grew with the Beatles as Pied Pipers leading the way.
I harnessed the energy of my generation and allowed it to carry me.
I was electrified by Bob Dylan (to this day)
In time I joined Sgt. Pepper's Lonely Hearts Club Band and
walked on the carpet of the Magical Mystery Tour.
The Beatles came to perform at a hockey rink called "Maple Leaf Gardens"
Several of the neighbourhood girls went. They stayed by the back door until Paul McCartney came out to light a cigarette and threw the book of matches to the girls. One caught it and brought it to school the next day.
She tore off the paper matches and gave me one.
I kept it in my wallet until I was past 50 years of age.
It was a reminder of a great time in history.
Whether anyone believed it was McCartney's, I don't know.
It didn't matter. I knew.

I opened the portals of my mind
I learned to love John as I would a personal mentor,
especially because he came to love Yoko and bring her to more prominence.
Yoko was a singular inspiration for this Miss General Idea of 1970.

John was the walrus. Oop oop ee doo

George chiselled into my narrow-minded approach to music with his Wonderwall Music.

Ringo endeared himself to all of us with humour and amazing time keeping.

And then there was Paul, the cute one. His lyricism was in a league with Gershwin,
Kern, and he was of MY generation.

Hair grew out and longer. It was a statement. It was defiant and courageous.
It was work keeping hair clean, but the hair was important – for the afros and the
sylphs and the hippie chicks and the mods and rockers and for all of us.

They came, they saw, they affected my heart.

A little piece of me is still spurred by Beatlemania
A big piece of me is still swirling in the gifted energy of Beatlemania.
And for that, they have "All My Lovin".

White Tangerine

Ron Smith

Humid night, humiliation of victory,
fame, they said, we had won. Coach Tom
stifled our elevator joy, looked at us
with those not-quite-dead eyes, said,
It's a good night, isn't it? And that
was that.

            My family had driven down
for the game, more family than anybody knew,
my secret wife there with my parents, a little knot
of tight praise, happiness restrained
after the Big Game.

                        She and I alone, came upon it
in the drug store's dazzling light, their latest,
astonishingly white, empty of imagery, just itself, just
the world, plain and white, just like us. We didn't know
Ringo had quit (and come back) or that so many
tracks were solo because of smoldering tangles,
we ourselves complexly in love, launching
ourselves blind into the future's chaos.
We hadn't yet read *Moby Dick*, had thought
lonely hearts was simply the apex, the way
everything had to be. And then she and
the game and a revolution whiter than sperm.

Timothy Leary had killed Brian E., scoured
the universe clean for love. The world was
our apple, I was a bleeding missile, hurtling
down the field on the Suicide Squad, happier
in mayhem than in tenderness, more hara-kari

than Maharishi. Then she, with her bottomless eyes
and perfect pelvis, was the world to come, sleepy
Orlando our Rishikesh, Richmond our Kinfauns.
How obliviously we plow our furrows!

                                        I was on my way
to Vietnam, surely, fatherhood, depression, and much worse,
so much to do, so many pages, papers, poems, songs,
we coming together, they flying apart, young people,
old people everywhere daring to eat the peach, tangerine
debris all over their faces, stickiness running down . . .

And Geoff Emerick, now we know—Ha!—hated
the stuff! We showed our blank parents the
so-called White Album, said, This is the best
thing that has ever happened, lifted needles
carefully over the road where nobody would care
in the future that we were doing it like dogs.
It was the Beatles the way we were
Mr & Mrs Smith, hidden in the plain sight
of Melville's disguisement and abasement—then
chastisement, then basement, even a Keatsean
casement in a neogothic dorm. Orlando
was cold later that week, rabbits, I'll betcha,
limped trembling through the frozen grass.

What about the Tangerine Bowl? my father said.
That was a football game, I said, she said, That
was a game. This is the world.

                                    My father's eyes, my
mother's: Not so much puzzled as searching. Somebody
might have said, That is a nothingness. Everythingness,

I thought at the time, should look like nothingness.
I was right, I was wrong. Parents all dead, so many
of my teammates, and both of us alive, carrying old
aches into a new century—I cover this page with words,
this white page . . .

O Classical dance-hall country,
cluster-bomb of genres, buzzard-fuck of romanticironic
you-name-it! It was a double album, just like us, double
everything, fitting together the way only flying
apart can. Hamilton, after Sgt. Pepper's seeped away,
of course, from Versailles fountains, let's say, to Salt Flats.
Who was the boss? Paul was, I was, embossed on our youth.
We were the greatest wrong righters since Schubert,
settled into marriage, found our way by losing it,
we, too, pretentious and frivolous, conservative and radical,
together and oh so flying apart. We were glass onions,
pampered piggies.

When they brought him to me, our son
had blood on his head. He squalled night after night
in the unairconditioned apartments. The world, afire with joy,
went right on burning itself down.

Summer 1965

Keith Inman

Coach spewed blood and guts, and foot-
ball was war, since he lost part
of something back in Nam. "CRUSH
your opponent!" he said, and lined up

across from a mop-top sub, and crushed
him into mud. "That is what it's about.
Boys!" His grey, bristled head glistened

with sweat. He pointed at a young, slit-eyed
foreigner, second string corner-back
of a limp-wrist hippie. "Next," Coach said,
and crushed the sod chewing punk

into earth. "Weak. Like this society.
Now, stand, again! Or, be crushed,
Hippie boy." Yan spat grass
through his mouth guard. "You got

no equipment." Coach ignored him,
crouched on all fours as Yan spread
his feet, cushioned his knees...at the wheel
of the whistle he locked his legs and drove

his fore-arm up-and-through Coach's
face. Mashed, bloodied, eyes bulging,
Coach rolled on the ground trying to see
"wha'tha'fuck" just happened. Yang

sparked his spikes across the asphalt.
Threw his helmet, jersey and pads
on the bench and pulled on his hall clicking
leathers, to slam a field of uprights.

Cool (1)

Roger Bell

As I walk uptown to get coffee cake at Ella Bolander's bakery, I pass by Henry's Men's Clothing. And stop. In the window he has fitted on a mannequin flared green tweed herringbone pants and a Paisley patterned shirt to match. My heart flips! Carnaby Street comes to this tiny town, I think, and forgetting the coffee cake, march right in.

Henry is sitting at his desk in the little office at the back, smoking. I like Henry. He has a moustache, is a dapper dresser. I think he fits the word debonair. He stands up when he sees me, sets the cigarette carefully in an ashtray, steps out between the maroon curtains that give his office some privacy. I tell him what I am interested in, he smiles, nods, goes in search of a pair of the pants and a shirt in my size. "You'll want this too," he says, handing me a wide belt with a huge ornate buckle. When I come out of the change room, stand in front of the mirror, I can't stop smiling. I am a Mod, straight off TV, with my high collar and big stiff cuffs, with my trendy flares. I already have Beatle boots so now I am complete.

I have Henry cut the tags off, put my old clothes in a bag, and I wear my outfit home. "Where's the coffee cake?" is all my mother demands when I walk in the door. Crap. I'll have to go back, but that's not so bad, I'll get the chance to strut all the way uptown. "Forgot," I say, "but I'll go back. Mom, what do you think of this?" She glances over from where she is setting the dining room table. "Nice," she says distractedly, goes back to folding napkins and setting out cutlery. She's having people for dinner and can't focus on me.

I need someone to. So I go next door where Larry and four of his friends who are starting a band are flailing away at their craft. His mom is sitting out in a lawn chair, her eyes half-shut, her face towards the sun. She has her glasses in her hand and I can see a red mark across the bridge of her nose where they fit too tightly. "Such bloody noise," she says, jerks her thumb towards the house. "I couldn't stand it any longer, I had to get out from the midst of that. I hope they get better. Soon." It isn't noise to me. Music has more and more become like breathing, and I go eagerly in, occupy a far corner, listen to a somewhat ragged but still propulsive version of Talahassee Lassie; they stop, there is much gesticulation, and heated discussion of how the drums and bass are out of synch. Larry, scowling, turns towards me, and as he does, his face lights up. "Cool!" he yells, "VERY cool." He rushes over to finger the collar, exclaim over the big flares. "You are so Mod, Roger." The others, less overtly, also admire my gear. He and his band-mates are three years older. I want their approbation. They are almost a band, and that is the epitome of cool. If someone cool says I'm cool, I am.

I listen some more, then I leave, head for Ella's, do a peacock walk-about, strut my stuff, singing a personalized version of the Manfredd Mann song: "Here I am just a-walkin' down the street, singin' doo wah diidy diddy dum diddy doo." My flares swish and the coffee cake is fragrant, still warm inside its paper bag. I anticipate how sweet that first slice will taste.

Run For Your Life

Ronnie R. Brown

Were the girls in her dorm nudging and
winking when they set her up
on that blind date? Remembering it
now, so many years later, she
knows they probably were, but
back then she thought they
were being kind. "He's, ya know,
Byronesque, very romantic, even has
a scar on his cheek ... except for that
he's a dead-ringer for George Harrison!"

At first, the date went well. Dinner
at a nice place, talk of poetry, but
when they started back things
changed. Sitting in his car outside
her dorm—the engine idling, radio
playing—he began to ramble: told her
his job was dealing
drugs; that he needed an
understanding, giving girlfriend.
Then he leaned in for a kiss
(she'd expected this, was leery now
but still willing). As they kissed,
the Beatles started to sing "You better run
for your life if you can little girl ..." and he
grabbed her left arm, twisted it hard
behind her then paused. "Shit," he said,
"I just love this song." And so they sat—
him holding her arm, John singing lead, Paul
and George joining in (later this song
would be banned from the radio stations,
but that was still decades away.)

The song ended and he twisted the arm a bit
more, said, "Tell me you love me!" She sat
numb; he twisted harder. "Yes, yes, of course!"
she said, nodding, enthusiastically. "Right!"
he smiled. "In the end they all do." Then
he sighed, released her arm and
heeding the advice of *the fab four*
she ran for her life.

Twiggy

Laurie Smith

Leslie do we blame you
big-eyed pixie micro-mini
Mary Quant clothes hanger for
Vogue international a luscious
adolescent androgen we devoured
like lunchbox pretzels, traded Keds
for gogo boots we painted on
eyelashes and measured our own
wrists against your vital statistics
publicly flaunted flatly and donned
bad Cockney accents learned all the
words to "Downtown" argued over
which Beatle we would marry,
who would marry such a fat chick in
reality?

We learned bad words like calorie,
Virginia Slim and statuesque, we told
in secret how to stick your fingers down
your throat and chewed on peanut butter,
Ayds reducing plan for breakfast drank
our diet cola, Metracal or vodka laced
with Dexatrim all remedies for ugliness.
We bought into magazines the tv ads
the weight and height charts posted near
mall dressing rooms with three-way mirrors
badly lit to sell us down a size in numbers
based on designer names or country, 5 petite
will cost you dearly, but who the hell
could wear a zero anyway?
We argued less material should be cheaper,

zero is a little girl who disappears behind
the looking glass, a slender wisp of
nothingness.

But Leslie aren't you doing
famously at 60-plus, still air-brushed, lean
and wealthy as a well-invested icon, judging
swimsuit competitions, cutting records for
the easy listening crowd and lending your
caché to Marks & Spencer, HSN and
Olay eye cream;
can we blame you?

My Coming of Age

I.B. Iskov

The Beatles belonged to me
in my coming of age.
It was a freer time
even though the Viet Nam war was raging,
even though there was unrest in the Middle East,
even though my parents were constantly fighting,
I had my Beatles record
to keep me safe and happy
when they sang "All You Need Is Love"

John, Paul, George and Ringo were all in love with me
in my coming of age.
It was a new time
even though psychedelic drugs were a problem,
even though organized crime was very organized,
even though I was failing math and geography,
I had my Beatles record
to assure me the world was a wonderful place
when they sang "Strawberry Fields Forever".

Every song by the Beatles was my favourite
in my coming of age.
It was a happy time
even though civil rights leaders were assassinated,
even though racism and anti-semitism were strong,
even though I was made to feel like a pariah at school,
I had my Beatles music
to make me feel wanted and cared about
when they sang "I Need You".

The Beatles were my closest friends
in my coming of age.
It was a flowery time
even though the threat of nuclear war hung over our heads,
even though there was mass murder world wide,
even though bullies threw stones at me
after school every day because of my lazy eye,
I had my Beatles to comfort and love me
every time they sang "Something".

Something is Happening Here

Betsy Struthers

For a week I've argued, Sis has argued, but Mom has made up her mind: I have to go with them when her new boyfriend takes her to Yorkville. *What kind of chaperone is a sixteen-year-old*? Sis yells, and Mom says, *better than none*.

I wear my new paisley shirtdress and the poncho I made from cutting a neck hole in a brown wool blanket. Sis is dressed in black: sweater, mini skirt, gogo boots. *Don't say a word*, she hisses when his car turns into the drive. Mom stands in the living room doorway, her thin lips thinning. Sis answers his knock and is already gone, the two of them rushing out to the car where they sit with the radio blaring, and *what's going on*? Mom demands, tweaking the curtains. They come back in and he says, *sorry, it's a song I've wanted her to hear, they don't play it often*. Sis is blushing, I am too. His hair is dark and Ringo long, a wisp of beard, peace medallion, leather jacket, pointed shoes. I watch Mom take inventory, but all she says is *don't stay out too late, you know your curfew*. Sis rolls her eyes.

His car is a blue Corvair with speakers mounted in the back so I can't hear what they say over the sound of "White Rabbit" and then "Purple Haze". His hand on the wheel has three silver rings, his other hand plays with a lock of Sis's hair. My own scalp tingles, my hands clasp tightly under the poncho. He parks on a street of thin redbrick rowhouses. *My pad*, he says, *come in just a minute*. Though this is against the rules.

He and Sis head upstairs, leave me in a hall littered with boots and bikes. Through an arch, candles flicker as Dylan drones on about Mr. Jones. A couple lie knotted on cushions below crimson velvet drapes.

The guy sits up, naked from the waist. *Hey man*, he says, *what's cooking*? When I shrug, not knowing what to say, he leans over to light his pipe. *Want to trip*?, he asks, and I answer, *Me? Where to*?, picturing Greece or California, a beach, palm trees, flowers. *Far out,* he says, *far out*. Sinks back into pillows, her stifled giggles.

Sis and her boyfriend clatter back downstairs. He's now wearing a denim jacket embroidered with daisies and mushrooms. Her hair is tousled, sweater rucked loose.

Around the block, a man in a tie-dyed caftan rocks on bare heels, fists raised, eyes closed, chanting to the streetlight. I skirt past him, follow boyfriend and Sis into a cellar beneath a record store. The smokey dark. Wedge into a booth at the back, boyfriend sandwiched between us. Waittress wears a shirt so gauzy thin I can't help but see her nipples. Try not to stare. Boyfriend orders. My first cup of cappucino. My first live music show: singer slouches on a stool, croons about clouds. Long blonde hair, bell bottoms, red guitar.

It's hot and I'd like to take the poncho off but my dress will look silly here among the turtlenecks and jeans. Some people nod their heads, not always keeping time, others share a cigarette. Sis rests her head on boyfriend's shoulder, her fingers playing with his pendant, his on her breast, I quickly look away. *Be back in a minute,* she says, getting up, leaving me alone with him.

His finger slides slowly down my arm, tickles my palm. *Little sister,* he murmurs, leaning close, his lips so close his breath burns my cheek. A shiver in my bones. *Hey,* Sis says. I shove him away, her away, stumble through the staring crowd, run down the street, dodging the hands that would grab me (Mom says) and stuff me with needles and pills.

A bus grinds to a stop and I board, slump in the seat behind the driver all the long way home. There, I sneak into the backyard, to Sonny's fort under the leafless lilacs, watch the lights turn off downstairs and up.

I have to wait for Sis to get home so we can go together into the house where Mom lies in bed, not sleeping, waiting. Sis never asks why I left. I never tell.

Elly's Birthday

Maureen Korp

On her birthday
Elly smoked gold-tipped cigarettes,
we all smoked then, but
Elly's cigarettes, her outrageous cigarettes
coloured pink, green, turquoise. . .?
she bought them on the street, someone said

I recall her wearing that heavy caftan from Rabat
last year's Berber souvenir. . . whenever that was
Elly's good at that, really good
improvising glee
her independent travels a model for us all

the perfect feminist, no option ever missed
"keeping her face in a jar by the door," we teased
but, I swear I heard her growl even as she smiled
when all the candles were lit,
when we sang our chorale for her:
"Stop it. Sisters. Peace, love, all that crap,
who's got time for it?
40 years, now that's a bloody bitch."

Playing the Beatles backwards

Robert Priest

Sometimes the Beatles
Broke Yoko Ono up

She said so
She said she loved

The way they made
Her laugh

Three Brother Melody

Deborah Cox

Finger-memorized the chords to *Ob La Di* at the age of twelve
played a song with friends, first band; what a show they made
hands upon the throat of a Gibson SG that his older brother lent him
Tom, the eldest, teaching both younger brothers their harmony
a lacquered dark brown body, rosewood neck, chrome tuning pegs
it was a beauty they all agreed, then harmonized more – *The White Album*
all friends, a reverb amp, and song

talked with hands since words failed in his throat as the doctor intoned
their newborn second son would not live, he simply died in his arms
such a small boy with the sheen of new pink skin, dark-pooled eyes
tiny fingers to grasp his father's clenched fist of a throat that could not
utter the symphony of life which had eddied so suddenly; a beauty he was
and would have certainly sung like his two grieving uncles –
all song and laughter and family

strummed *Blackbird*, his youngest brother's favourite at his unforeseen
funeral, packed to the rafters with friends and family because Don,
full of stories and too much booze and always the laughter, somehow
found a crowd gathered 'round, guitar cradled in his hands, a veritable
one-man show; his last guitar, a Tak, red sunburst, dreadnought shape
its sound bright to match the acoustics of his life –
all beauty and song and family

wrote on parchment with ink his older brother's last wishes, the song
in his throat stopped, cancer silenced both vocals and tongue, but not
the chords — vibrant with lyrics and life, warm mid-range tones of his prized
Washburn, tobacco-warm brown, sunburst finish, fingerboards near-hollow
he hammered the shit out of all the frets, Gibson and South American
nylon strings — hard on them, they were meant to be played, like his life –
all laughter and family and song.

Ornithologists believe "the laughing seagull" is laughing at blackbirds for that stupid Beatles song about them.

David McGimpsey

C'mon. When I say I "hate" the Beatles
don't get me wrong. I don't mean it that way.
I just mean that I have a disliking
for their horrible, horrible music.

When I think of the Beatles hit songs –
from "Oopie Doopie Bee" to "O Deirdre",
from "Mrs Medwin's Sunday Chutney"
to "Step Right Up, Sidney Dear" – I wince.

Not because their songs are poorly written
or performed in an inadequate fashion.
For a group so drug-addled they could not
perform live, the Beatles made hit records.

It just makes me wince. Maybe that's just me.
I've seen people singing classic Beatles songs –
from "Hey, Moon Cat!" to "Love Is So Lovely" –
and they all seemed perfectly happy to me.

All My Loving

Bruce Meyer

It is 10:15 on December 8th
and we still believe we will live forever.

I am pretending what it is
to kiss the lips I am missing
through the taste of beer and undergrad nights
as snow falls on the Morrisey Tavern
and Bloor Street is barely traveled.

It is 10:15 on December 8th
and I imagine how to change the world.

The Patriots have tied the game
and Cosell's prattle drones like winter.
I want to find the words for magic,
the courage of poets to live for love,
to learn what the heart is and what it feels
and how brief candles shine for us
when they light a path we cannot see.

It is 10:15 on December 8th
and all of us are still young forever.

I smile at the squeaky mattress springs
of a friend's bed dancing beneath us,
five year olds twisting and shouting,
though gently, so the needle won't skip
on the birthday forty-fives
his gran posted from the 'Pool
with instructions for boys to keep their hair short.

But 11:07 stops the heart.
A knife in the hour makes time a beast.
I emerge from the subway to see my breath
and men weeping like New York rain;
the sky is falling and my coupled footprints
are marks on time I must leave behind.

And somewhere in a Redeemer's room
the muzak promises to always be true
and I listen, eyes blind, to weep for you.

Up in Smoke

Tell me if you if you were not happy in those days
You-five
And you had not yet abandoned the guitar
Donald Justice
On the Night of the Departure by Bus

Elizabet Stevens

We made our rules
broke the boxes of containment
travelled with no baggage
took many trips
to the corner store and beyond
drank the wine of wonder
Tell me if you were not happy in those days.

We were born again and again
Preached the gospel of St. Martin in the Fields
(because we liked the name)
sang to "Lucy in the Sky with Diamonds"
prayed for peace
found love in the mud
shed tears of redemption
even the old were young again
You were not yet twentyfive.

We caressed the gold of our ambition
roamed the forests barefoot and spangled
talked and talked and talked again
around a campfire of burning change
slept on a bed of hollyhocks and thyme
so much to do
And you had not yet abandoned the guitar.

Something Other Than Jesus

I'm not saying that we're better or greater,
or comparing us with Jesus Christ ...
– John Lennon

Andreas Gripp

Not all will sing the anthem
when it's scribed,
that *All You Need is Love*

and there is no love
when records smash and burn
and vinyl has a sickly smell
and ghostly smoke
and hate is heard in stereo,
that *Old Time Religion*
where fire sets the heretics
alight,

we with effeminate hair
unshorn,
our women donning pants,
their naked breasts bouncing
to our fleshly beat of sin,
we who know nothing of a love
that lies in its own blood
outside us.

Song

Don Gutteridge

It was the decade of the damned,
the side streets littered
with hippies, while freedom riders
braved lynch mobs
and fear-mongers in the deep
embittered South, and then
some mad malcontent
put a bullet through the un-
stoppable heart of Martin
Luther King, while off
in a California kitchen
Bobby was dropped by an
assassin's gun, and all
the while the music soared:
Dylan and Lennon and a dozen
troubled troubadours
who sang our grief, our out-
raged anger, our need
for the lift of a lissome lyric—
as if the songs themselves
would be world enough.

Lennon Backwards by bed

Robert Priest

I

She lies back flat on the bed
Fully dressed
Her gaze, her arms away from him.
He's naked on his side, pressed against her
One long leg, bent across her chest
His arm and wrist
Framing and holding her face

Just as his lips touch her cheek
Annie Liebowitz clicks
It's voted the world's all-time #1 magazine cover
It's his last morning on earth

II

Their peace ad and honeymoon
Bed-in bed
Where journalists
Lie down with them
For interviews
The bed they share with her daughter
With celebrities
And TV crews
Selling non-violence like soap

From this bed he sings
"Give Peace A Chance"
In a great raw holler
And it's a world-wide hit

III

A very Jesus-looking man rolls a hospital bed
Into Abbey Road studio
His lover in it recovering from a car crash
"We can't bear to be apart,"
He tells the other Beatles.
They're annoyed but go ahead
Their final album recorded in the presence of this bed

IV

After a gig
Two motherless men
Enter a hotel room

Face to face
On the ends of twin beds,
A lefty and a righty
They finish off their first American Number one
She loves you
To synchronize the harmonies
They lean in close
And watch each other's lips

V

"Out of this rock"
Is the motto of the school
The schoolboy hates
He'd rather lie in bed all day and float upstream
Aunt Mimi calls him lazy
An underachiever
But he knows already he's got something
Though he's never even heard of rock and roll.

VI

Age three, his mother
Lets him sleep with her
In the same bed as her lover
Aunt Mimi reports them
Aunt Mimi steals him from that bed
To which he can never find his way back

VII

1942
Incendiaries fall on Liverpool all night long
The worst raid of the war and newborn John
For safety's sake
Is placed beneath the bed.
Beneath the bed his first night on earth Lennon screams
That great raw holler in fine form
as the bombs roar

Time-slide to Joy

Katherine L. Gordon

In this mean era
where war and corruption rule,
we turn to the Mind's Treasure Book
to hear the music of peace and love,
a thumping ribaldry of fun and joy
that lost word "hope" a beat repeating,
echoes of Beethoven's ode
in an ever-youthful harmony
to make us smile, tap light feet
in a freedom feeling we thought faded,
the gift of the Beatles, those Liverpool boys,
who may not have known their special destiny,
but in that group of four,
guitar knights at the world's table
we find the chords that might
unite us afterall.

The Devil Walked Past Us As We Sat By The Mississippi

Amber Homeniuk

us, Max Witchdoctor coated in pyramids and eyes
the Bee Pollen Princess all flowers and beaded hair
High Priestess SaRa, jewelled and feathered in blue sky
and clouds shaped a hand pointing us out in purple and orange ecstasy
though later we would say it was only orange
we felt him coming

in slow motion boardwalk creaking boots he was coming
sun stagnated, river dimmed, leaves stilled – touched by his eyes
his the only movement coat tails lifting flames in his orange
flapping trousers flames in glassy eyes and orange hair
his heavy swinging fisted arms his raging yellow ecstasy
bigger than the sky

he sucked all the bruised colours from the aching sky
blew back clouds past seeping sun oh yeah he was coming
every tread of his soles gripping releasing gripping the boards
        was ecstasy
us too afraid gripping releasing to close our eyes
against him come so near we felt his breath mat our hair
and our eyes froze open while everything went misty orange

orange lampposts orange foghorns I dreamt I was eating an orange
touching Max touching SaRa all my beads floating off into the sky
could see his whorled ears dripping chin every strand of hair
and we were petrified that he was coming
seeking us with hate-filled eyes
we knew he was coming and it was ecstasy

through gaps in threads out every pore leaked skin-hot ecstasy
he hated it so hard his eyes streamed orange
he was right up close furious into our eyes
screaming, oh how he despised us being beneath that sky
and our chanted charm, *God bless John Lennon*, when we heard him coming
panting and snarling to the edges of his crackling clothes and hair

so angered that all he could do was wind-blast our hair
jealous of us locked together in ecstasy
unable to join or break it, even with his coming
he didn't realize he'd scared us orange
and seared the very colours of the sky
he would own nothing of us, we saw it in his eyes

we trailed his hair toward Jackson Square, receding blur of orange
turning in ecstasy on our bench under shimmering New Orleans sky
where he backbent the Mississippi, coming and gone before our eyes

The night I heard the news of John Lennon's assassination, my baby son Dylan was asleep in his bedroom at the top of the stairs, my unborn son Sean was seven months in the womb, and I was gently weeping at the shock of it. Wife Cathy came home from an evening out, to find me teary and ashen, sitting on the couch, the TV newsman recounting the horrifying details. What a waste! To this day, I refuse to utter the murderer's name aloud. And I still find it hard to speak of the loss I felt then, the deep loss I still feel to this day.

John B. Lee

Dec. 8, 1980

Robert Priest

I think John Lennon is falling
He takes two steps, two more steps
and a hole opens in the earth
five holes in the earth
and John Lennon is falling
Falling from my childhood
Falling from the earth
Two steps he takes
Two more steps
and then he falls face forward
We can't believe it
He falls through our arms
through our tears
We might be ghosts for all we can do
to stop him
He falls from a thousand buildings
in a huge rain of bodies
They are shooting him out of the skies
shooting him in San Salvador
shooting him in Santiago
Lennon's blood flows into the Hudson
It flows down the Mississippi
A red tide reaches Britain's shores
His blood soaks into the setting sun
He stains the Japanese coast
John Lennon is falling out of the sky
saying one last thing to us

his eyes wide
his lips moving
saying one last thing
we can’t quite hear
It is too sudden
The earth opens
There is a hole in the sky
five holes in heaven
and Lennon is falling out of sight
into the sky
smashing into the earth
first one foot
then the other foot
just two steps
just two more steps
and then he falls face forward
into our arms
deep into the world
Lennon falls

Decade

On the loss of John Lennon

Bill Howell

The starter shakes hands with time
to get on home. The windshield discovers flakes
with quick deaths, uncovers moth thoughts
melting into the car's forehead. At the very centre of
the hard core, we stayed at it long after we wore out the knees
on the pants of our breath. But how could anybody start
to understand the kind of people who actually planned to be 40
while you were busy refusing to be 20 and everybody
was suddenly old enough to be held responsible?

I mean like it's a blast from the past & I can understand
how you could miss some of the lyrics, reinventing them
enough to keep the tune going. But what if
you never picked up on them the first time around? Moths
beating moth brains out trying to get in,
while the wipers beat out the time with the song
slowly dissolving into the radio weather.

Beyond the city's breathing limits, there's something
every love song lover is obliged to provide alone.
Now this instant, placeless voice – a static absence of silence
lost in licensed distance. This is the quest lost in myth,
the truth left over from prayer. While white moth wind
fills in & smoothes out what's left of the street.

Imagine

Mary Ann Mulhern

John Lennon's handwriting
First draft of *Imagine*
In a wooden frame
For sale

His words shape a world
We share in peace
His voice sings above bullets and bombs
In cold refugee tents
Solitary cells

Who can possess
Imagine?

More of us join
Borrow the pen
Of a dreamer
Trace every letter

Imagine

I of Death

Keith Inman

Padmavati waited at the green
light as cars
moved slowly through the red.
Her long nails tapped the steering
wheel to the refrain
of Lennon's "Imagine".
Maddy
would be so furious
if Paddy were late.
A loud blast
bruised the air behind her.
A silver Caddy
veered into the blind lane, cut
in front of her,
spangling her grill with stones.
The mad-dashed
purple-fumed rage
severed the flagged procession,

a blade of sun sliced the world
in half.
The driver waved for Paddy
to go too, if she really needed to,
but Paddy
let go of the wheel and raised
her palms.
A child in the back seat stared.

Dwayne

Keith Inman

Main Street's line of classics
gleamed, hood-raised above
chrome, orange, and lime green
blocks as ball-capped buffs
worried about clouds in the east.

Heads turned at each
polished fender: 49 Hudson,
57 Belair, 69 Cuda, 81 Bronco,
09 Honda...a Honda!

The foreigner slow paraded up Main
passed Homestead Hardware
where Roger's Roadster sat angled
to the curb belting out the best
of the Beatles between a red Corvette
and yellow Corvair.

Roger turned to Dwayne,
"Who the fuck let the rapper
in?" Dwayne pulled himself
out of his canvas chair beside the table
full of nodding bobble-heads
and jumped into his 73 camouflaged
RoadRunner and rumbled up
the ole V8, strafing the beige Civic
with red-line revolutions as lightning
raced the crowd for cover.

5 July, 2013: Four Copts killed outside Luxor, in Dab'iya Village, Egypt

Maureen Korp

We lay them
one by one
heads wrapped round, swaddled under the chin,
closing the mouth keeps it closed,
in death, you see
jaws drop open
in death
air pushes out of the lungs,
sometimes we hear them shouting
sometimes they gurgle, too
we close their mouths, then no one will hear
another sound from the dead

The eyes of the dead are always closed,
yet they're not ever sleeping
they die with open eyes
every one of them trying to see what's coming next
we close their eyes when they die,
no one wants to know what the dead are seeing

That's just how it is.

Those men are fastening four into place
onto boards, holding them flat,
putting them into the ground,
white-shrouded Copts, poor souls
each with a paperback book on their breast
the covers are icons of Jesus reborn, like Osiris before

O writer, make something of this

Can't buy me love, 1964

Maureen Korp

the pearls were fakes
    good fakes, fake nonetheless

the emerald?
    glass
    CocaCola glass. Something any fool could see, but you

Can't buy me love. Can't sing the tune?

    money, honey, that's what I want
    money, honey

Much more I can do with that

Carnival of Lights

for Paul McCartney

John B. Lee

you speak of the deep fans
the ones who want
the soundscapes
every noise and breath you make
even someone drunkenly
stumbling into the drums
even the woozy
volumes of four drugged voices
chanting like mountain monks
even the unintelligible
rattle of all that
chain dragging and glass breaking
thump and thunder
recorded and unreleased
from long after
the time you recall
an early job
when you were
the second man on the lorry
sleeping in the seat
on a drive
after the loading in Liverpool
working for SPD—speedy prompt delivery
at a time when you and George
were just two adolescent lads
at the town dance
hard to imagine
you snoozing in that lorry
hard to imagine a young Beatle striking out
with the girls

now you say
you dream sometimes
of concerts
with the goers leaving
early, a line of
disappointed listeners
listlessly shuffling
a crowd of empty seats
as you sing
into an increasingly vacant hall
as though it were sound check

and you wake in a sweat
like any other man

feeling the cold fever
of ordinary anxiety

and you said—
the driver was a kind man
who let you nap
on the journey
between departing and arriving
and he woke you
for the unloading

his kindness remembered
might keep them in their seats
longer than dreaming ...

Another One Gone

Denis Robillard

I'm thinking of a Bukowski
poem called
Where The Writers?
and churn some famous names in my mind
trying to account for oceans of words written
countless poets lost in the widening stream.

I think of singers
gone too, gone and sunk
their brain tunes now only writ in water.

While I too sink into
the soft landscape
of Warsteiner beer cans
slumped across the carpet.

I'm thinking about the human element of this planet
a billion births
and a faded Beatles' poster
on the wall.

Tonight I think of
those young Turks,
each long-haired Adonis
who shook the foundations of music
with their locks
and hipsway guitar.

This year alone, the Fisher King prankster Ken Kesey
has gone for the last boat ride
following Garcia down the river of Forgetfulness to
Acid heaven.

Purdy and Richler riding in that same damn skiff;
the quiet Beatle riding shotgun
his light extinguished tonight.

While rain on rain on rain convulses this city into chaos.

Goethe at the Airport

John B. Lee

I had almost entirely forgotten how at a stopover
in the airport lounge in Hamburg
I had sat on a stool beside Goethe
in the ersatz café sipping cold lager, eating a stale sandwich
my wife nearby
the small foam on my flat beer forming a sudsy circle
soaping the top of my glass like a dishwasher's regret
we were on layover on our way to Tel Aviv
the sky above Europe ashy that summer with
Grimsvotn's terrible eruption
canceling flights, rerouting air traffic
we were also worried by Arab spring
the ruined excursions on the Nile
this traveling joyful lamentation
I was thinking of the band in 1961
the hot little combo
at the Kaiserkeller in the Pauli Quarter
and of Stu Sutcliffe's heartbroken pal
receiving the news of his death, how
eternally youthful the dying are
when they die young and are dead forever
I've seen his dark canvas blackened with paint
the raw red energy
the pain of it sharp as a stick in the eye
and Astrid's grief in those sepia-tone photographs
of burnt-out streets of that German city after the war
and I remember the Christmas carols of my childhood
I recall the journey of the magi and Handel's Messiah
all imaginary snow deep in the depths of the day
and here, the bitter flavour of warm amber
tainting the taste of these words
waiting as we were to take flight

to climb into the clear air
piercing the volcanic overcast
seeking blue heaven high above the horrors of history
nearly impossible to believe
the pewter-pale forehead of the poet
the hollow knock of his metallic hat
how once, skating in Germany
he had imagined
the ice forever trackless in his path

Beatle Love

Terry Ann Carter

It doesn't surprise anyone in Montreal
that haiku poet Marco Fraticelli is a Beatles fan:

the man has affinity for insects
writes about melting spring and magpies

and boxes of Kleenex on the school teacher's desk —
also has a hankerin' for the famous four

knowing those keyboard chords, as he does,
for gigs in Florida with the Club Med set.

New Year's Eve and it's all *Michelle,*
and *Sgt. Pepper, A Hard Day's Night.*

Marco, grinning behind the strobe lights
tossing them out like spins of the hula hoop

twisting and shouting down the dance floor
another round of *Love, Love Me Do*

then *Here Comes the Sun*, closes
his eyes to sing *Don't Let Me Down,*

Hey Jude, All the Lonely People,
all the while composing his next small poem

about nudist camps, an aquarium light,
his grumbling stomach, or worms on the sidewalk.

A Glass Onion

Anna Yin

Well, John, you must understand
I was a little girl then
behind walls of silence
at a remote town in the Oriental world.
Skipping stones on a soundless river,
I have missed ripples of the outer world
for decades.

Now your loyal fans fill me in with your legends.
They regret that the ruthless bullet took your life.
Yet looking through a glass onion,
everything is still there, your music, your love
and your *Hello, Goodbye*..
I cannot help but cry.

John, I have arrived—
not only in your songs, but also in your epic world.
Yet thirty years have passed,
I open an enormous clam,
no pearl left, neither *Mr. Moonlight*.
I cannot help but cry.

Through *the strawberry fields,*
upon the bent backed tulips
into the other half lives
the long and winding road
across the universe
love me do, love me do...
I see a fool on the hill
trying to make a dove-tail joint...

Looking through a glass onion,
everything is still there, your music, your love.
I cannot help but cry.

A Hard Day's Night on the Day of an Eclipse

Dylan Lee

On a day when the sun became an empyreal ring
a florid halo in a blinding sky
in the vast azure of endless circumstance
we three wore mesh-backed baseball caps
and walked with our father
to the video store
to conjure his heroes.
And after, in our house
the basement had carpet
the colour of an old orange tabby
seeking the heat of an idling engine.
My brother and I leaned back on our hands
like exhausted runners
our fingers splayed in the thickness of polypropylene
in the faded stickiness of grape juice spills
and the threadbare wounds of floor hockey.
We sat in front of the television set
and watched
men who could run as swift as trains
who played like children
and sang in the pitch of my father's heart,
who swam in the buoyant scream.
And again, we danced
on the infinite memory of music
while my brother strummed a plastic guitar
and I breathed a silent saxophone.

Summer in Detroit

Marty Gervais

A flimsy wooden seat
from Detroit's old Olympia
bought for $25
is the closest thing I have
to the Beatles
who played in that arena
once in 1964, again in 1966
and I think of my friend
who said it was nearly midnight
when their Greyhound pulled away
from the Olympia —
he could hear them singing *Long Tall Sally*
as teenage girls rushed after them into the street
to trail after the bus —
Cleveland bound, an all nighter
Someone said they heard their laughter
saw them wave from the open windows
a humid August night
swore they tossed their cufflinks
to frantic stretched out hands
my 18-year-old high school buddy
had skipped class
to hang out at the Whittier Hotel downtown
and dialed all day long a radio station
so he could win one square inch
of the sheets Lennon slept on
I don't know if any of it is true
I don't care — the broken down
seat from the Olympia rests
in a corner of my basement

I’m struggling to find some kind of metaphor
for how I should feel, some lyric moment
for this brush with greatness
as I sit down on that wooden chair
the hum of the furnace
in the silence of a summer afternoon
but this is nothing to compare
with the postage stamp-sized remnant
from John Lennon’s bed
that rests in a dresser drawer
in an envelope from the radio station

I swear I can hear someone sleeping

Fond of the Beatles

for John Winston Lennon

What can science teach us about the nature of God?
"I should say He was inordinately fond of beetles."
—JBS Haldane

Ron Charach

If I never wrote a poem about you,   it was because who could listen to a poem   above the explosive din of those screaming girls?   I never followed your tours the way my friend Mark did, he saw you play Ed Sullivan in 1964,   "me and how many other thousands of kids..."   then ran out to buy his first electric guitar.

Survive out there, pull you to me by your jetlag hair...

Do I keep this to myself, take John's advice:

Hey! You've got to hide your love away...

But your hair was wig-perfect,   "What do you call your haircut?" an American reporter challenged George,   "I call it Arthur."

And those beards gave you auras of holy men. Like Leonard Cohen, you had your own guru, a maharishi defrocked in "Sexy Sadie".

Just don't tell me that the double White Album was recorded in a studio, because each song created a world of its own.

Obladi, Oblada, life goes on, brah...

Blackbird singing in the dead of night...

You say you want a revolution...

Charles Manson heard special messages in the Revolution pieces, combined them with "Little Piggies" and "Helter Skelter", then led his 'family' to slaughter Sharon Tate, the baby inside her and four visiting friends.

The crescendo apocalypse in "A Day in the Life" in *Sgt. Pepper's* seems pale in comparison, though the chaotic noises in "The Walrus" are dark wonders, *goo goo ga joob!*

Sitting in an English garden waiting for the sun... If the sun don't come, you get a tan from standing in the English rain... ... Here comes the sun, Here comes the sun, and I say, it's alright...

Was my passion for gun control tweaked by *Happiness is a warm gun,* and *Hey, Bungalow Bill, what did you kill, Bungalow Bill...* then chambered by four hollow-point bullets burrowing into John Lennon's back?

Christ, you know it ain't easy, You know how hard it can be, yeah, The way things are going, they're gonna crucify me.

They say Mark David Chapman shot you for blasphemy, but no doubt he loved you, was inordinately fond.... he used the stopping power of his Charter Arms .38 special to draw closer, to forever marry his name to yours... once finished, he sat down on the side-walk, dropped the smoking gun and picked up the paperback, "Catcher in the Rye". It wasn't enough you had autographed his copy of "Double Fantasy" just hours before, that he had seen your nanny walking five-year-old Sean and remarked to her, "What a beautiful boy," or that photographer Fran Leibowitz photo-shot you that same morning, stretched out along Yoko's fully clothed body, in just your birthday suit. The concierge tore off your shirt and didn't know where to start, then removed your blood-stained, Oliver Goldsmith granny glasses.

All we are saying ... is give peace a chance.

1980, on a blind date in Manhattan I park outside John and Yoko's condo building, the Dakota. Being Canadian, I remember to lock the car doors. Hours later, we return, my date and I, to find the back windshield shattered to tiny glassy beads by a thief who smashed it with a huge construction block, for an old leather coat worth a hundred bucks at most. At the sight, Deborah exploded into laughter...

Bang, bang, Maxwell's silver hammer came down, on her head...

It's not easy to comment on the colossal duo, Lennon and McCartney. You had in common Liverpool roots and mothers lost early, Paul's to a blood clot, with John unloaded at age five to an aunt, his birth mother, years later, struck dead by a drunk driver.

Let me first remove Ringo, Richard Starkey, who got by with a little help from your friends, and an octopus's garden in the shade, before doing voices on *Thomas the Tank Engine* You went into a coma around first grade and spent a year in hospital while your father extended his pub crawl.

Survive out there! Pull you to me by your sweatband hair...

George Harrison, yours was a country estate lawn spirituality, you ripped off The Chiffons' "He's so fine", elevated as "My Sweet Lord". but bless you for *While my guitar gently weeps...*

Great Sir Paul, you could be the air in the souffle: *You'd think that people would have had enough of silly love-songs, I look around me and I seeee it isn't so! And what's wrong with that, I'd like to know, 'Cause here I go, a-gainnnn:*

I... love...you!...

author of the worst line ever: "*The willow turns its back on inclement weather*"... but bless you for leavening "In my life" and "Fool on the Hill". Your second wife turned you into a seal-pup activist; but what is an activist, just someone who takes what happens in the world personally…

John, we can only *Imagine* you on your own, since Yoko didn't let you out of her crosshair sights.

Survive out there; pull you to me by your long black hair.

I wish I were enough of a dancer to groove to "Twist and shout"… You made it big so early, in your twenties and thirties, then Yoko ambushed you with an adulthood full of lie-ins for peace… . You were meant to survive, not be extinguished, not to flame out like Jim Morrison, but to witness generations, like Mick Jagger and Keith Richards, like Bowie.

"There were five women that were my family," you wrote, "Five *strong, intelligent, beautiful* women, One happened to be my mother. (She) just couldn't deal with life." Other parents' warned their kids to steer clear of you, "I would infiltrate the other boys' minds, I would say, "Parents are not gods because I don't live with mine, and therefore, I know…"

Survive out there, pull you to me by your auburn hair…

Do I take aim at what, in a snit, I renamed "The Long and Winding Toad"? or semiautomatic ear worms like "Hey Jude", "Let it Be" and "All you Need is Love", when I prefer "Come Together", the words like something out of John's slender volume, in his own write:

Here come old flattop, he come groovin' up slowly *He got joo-joo eyeball, he one holy roller…* He bag production, He got walrus gumboot He got Ono sideboard, He one spinal cracker, He got feet down below his knees Hold you in his armchair, you can feel his disease…

Come together! Fab Four... over me...

Thanks, John, Paul, George and Ringo, in that order. I know what you mean by "A Hard Day's Night", and worked "Eight Days a Week" on hospital call, tried my luck as a "Paperback Writer", dreamed of being a working class hero, and while I never took LSD (yes, I know, "Lucy in the Sky with Diamonds" wasn't really about that), while on a whiff of Mary Jane, I caught a glimpse of the slow, stepwise descent into hell you captured in "I Want You (She's So Heavy)"...

She's so (–da-da-da-da-da, da-da-da-da-da) Heav-vyyyy, ooh....

And now that there's quiet, finally a little quiet, may I mix a few Wiki-facts with your volatile lyrics like primer meeting gunpowder in the casing of a poem that celebrates how you
dazzled, and knocked us all dead:

I was always waiting for this moment to arrive...

My Beatles! Bye-bye...

It's Raining

Paul Jeong

In the poem rain symbolizes the Beatles and the descending image of 60's culture along with its counterculture with the passage of time. The remaining background is 'hit' by rain, which implies influence on the cultural scene before the Beatles landing in America and the overall events in that era (Vietnam, black society, hippie culture, women's rights, etc.)

I hear it rain
on the crowd of crowns
on the forest, to the smallest leaf.

Feel it seep into every crevice
of every frame.

Hear the grasp and touch of every root
down to the wisps
even to the lowest footstep.

Cover continents
with the note of each drop
to blanket the wail of the wounded.

And wash away
to wash away forgotten deaths
to wash away the face
of distorted landscapes
shaped by tears.

Imagining silence
after the fall

total quiet

where eyes are opened
amid the awakening.

Lab Tech 8:22 a.m.

Ron Charach

Until you breeze in, flipping
back your ponytailed head, sporting
a pink clinical jacket with matching pink pants,
the waiting room is a morose collection
of souls awaiting tests, some covered
by the health plan, some not.

You may be late, but what a relief to your partner,
also a Philippina, caught up in some awkward tests on an infant,
screaming as it squirms on a table just beyond our sightlines.
You reel in the desk chair with your leg, then start typing
requisitions like the wind, springing
to greet me and sit me down, showing
not the least hesitation as you feel for,
then tap my finest vein, having thoughtfully asked,
Do you have a favorite arm?

From the moment you flick on
your golden oldies radio station,
we the waiting have a sense that maybe, just maybe,
we are in the right place, at the right time.
Before you, we had, as background music,
nothing but drab taupe decor, the tinkle of urination
from a washroom a thin sheet of drywall away,
and the cries of that baby being put
through its paces.

As you feel for my vein, you greet
a repairman who has wandered in,
then sweetly, ever so quietly, sing,
as you draw my blood:
I wanna hold your ha-a-a-a-a-and...
I wanna hold your hand...

Feeling not the least bit violated,
my own song centre spins,
She loves you, yeah, yeah, yeah
Nor do I even mind your needle
slipping into my personal space,
much as I, so early in the morning,
have entered yours...

Hey Jude the Obscure

Laurie Smith

Hey Jude the obscure,
Arabella was a manipulative
bitch but your beloved Susan
had issues way beyond your patience.
You were not meant to go out and get her—
Holy shit! How many brick walls should a man
slam his head against, the girl wouldn't even
put out, and all that blush and titter was likely
a cover up for unresolved transgressions way before
the teacher, or even Hardy himself
knew her.

You could never make it better, and sticking her
with a morose little orphan from your first marriage
was, although admirable, (spoiler alert)
a very bad idea in the end, *suffer the little children,*
hanging like washrags all in a row, planted like bastards
in the Victorian rain.

Oh, nowadays we wouldn't turn a head for natural marriage,
blended families out to enjoy the Sunday parade, but boy
it's still only an illusion; those unborn sons and daughters
heavy on your shoulders best be reconsidered
long before the destination wedding
drama, honeymoon rebuff and suitcase on the landing
three weeks in.

If, Jude, you had a mother—I would tell you
run away, your skin is thin and some women
are just not worth the effort.

First Dance

Ronnie R. Brown

"Now for the bride and groom's
first dance" the DJ announces and,
as the couple moves to the dance floor,
The Beatles begin to sing *When I get older,*
losing my hair... as the guests murmur
appreciatively. The guy on her left, whose wife
like her husband, seems more enthralled
with the remains of his cake, than the music,
says, "Perfect choice!" and she nods.

She wonders if he knows
that Paul was only sixteen
when he wrote that song. That John
hated it; thought it was "too Music
Hall," which was why it took till Sgt.
Pepper to get it recorded.

You'll be older too... The parents
have joined in now, the bride's father
swinging his kilt with gusto.

Sad, she thinks, back when they recorded
this song they were all so young
who would have believed that two of them
wouldn't live long enough to see
if someone would still be *sending...*
a Valentine. She's hardly noticed
her shoulders moving to the music
but the guy on her left has, so
when the DJ says "Let's play it again
so you all can join in!" he
grabs her by the hand

and they start dancing. "Hell,"
he shouts above the music,
"I could be 100 with a walker
and when they play the Beatles
I'll be waddling up to dance!"

That's when he twirls her
and, like the girl she used to be,
she wants the Beatles
to keep singing
forever.

Boys, Are You Buzzing?

John Tyndall

You're going to lose that group
yes, yes, you're going to lose
that group of limbs
once a smooth unit
like a seasoned band
left leg and foot
stamping out rhythm
in a Cuban-heeled boot
right leg and foot
driving the kick-pedal
bass-drum beat
left arm and hand
hitting an unstable chord
for an unstoppable song
right arm and hand
picking out a riff
ending in a Picardy third
all four members
playing together
and nothing
could touch them
but there's a new disease*
sweeping through you
and the break-up starts
at the very marrow
of your aging body
and the men in white
lab coats ask
if you feel the buzz
as the floor gives way
beneath your kit
and all the neurologists
and all the haematologists
can't put the group
back together again

* MGUS! b/w I'm Neuropathic

So Many of Us

John Wing

The Beatles stayed here, almost fifty years
ago, which has to be wrong, since so many
of us are still alive. I walked up 54th street
to the Ed Sullivan Theater. The boys were no
doubt driven the four blocks. Me no one noticed.

I was five years old that year. The older kids
discussed the band every minute, and bought
.45s as fast as they were shipped. There were
arguments too; screaming You-don't-know-shit-
about-George fights. Or Paul. Or John.

The front men seemed interchangeable then,
like spokes that shredded baseball cards. They
hadn't split into personality-camps yet. I liked
Ringo, because the girls adored him, and what a cool
thing, to be named Ringo. Bells on your toes...

My father hated the whole thing, called them
the Yeah Yeah Yeahs. It was tricky, because we
were still shaving together then. Our relationship
was only beginning to learn its limitations, so
the lads weren't mentioned at table or over sink.

But today might as well be the moon to then,
walking up 54th to Broadway, recalling the black-
and-white world of a half-century ago, when fame
was your goal but not your fault. Fame wasn't
business then. It was commitment.

Revs

John Tyndall

So I find myself
lost in suburban acres
roads laid out off
any grid in planning
ranch house after ranch house
no sidewalks, no gutters
no streetlights, no illumination
everything unfinished
lost, but here comes the light
from a 1966 Mini Cooper
and George Harrison rolls
down his driver's window
says, *Care for a lift, sailor?*
and I climb right in
settle back in black leather
telling him I dreamed of
Sgt. Pepper's Lonely Hearts Club Band
a dream I dreamed weeks before its release

So I find myself
in Mary's Record Mart
discovering in the Beatles' bin
the long-awaited album
looking on the back cover, all
one bright, solid colour
to see if it includes the songs
Strawberry Fields Forever
and Penny Lane, *searching*
through columns and columns
of words and more words
but nowhere can I locate them

George smiles and smiles and smiles
revs his magical Tantric motor
and drives me out of suburbia
so I find myself

The Cloud Album

Bruce Meyer

George Martin thought time away from the studio would do him good. The final days of the *Abbey Road* sessions had almost killed him and the debacle and character assassinations of the *Let It Be* recordings – the constant shifting from studio to studio to rooftop – had left him drained. Glyn Johns had taken over the mixing and editing for the aborted *Get Back* album that had been shelved in favor of *Abbey Road*. *Abbey Road* had led to more acrimony in the group. Paul wanted to tour and was threatening to quit. John wanted to stay home and off the road and called Paul a git. Ringo didn't know. The quiet Beatle played sour chords, but simply stared at his band-mates and wondered silently to himself how they had come so far since the days of Corn Flake diets in the garrets of Hamburg. How had they fallen so low as to despise each other? George Martin was burnt out and had had enough.

He was watching the stars from the glacis of a house he had rented in Anguilla when the phone rang. It was little George. Harrison was about the only one he wanted to see at that point. His quiet, shy demeanour was something that Martin found soothing. The time in India had made Harrison into an even quieter, and a more philosophical being. He had nothing to shout about. As the two Georges met at the door, the young Beatle said that he hoped he wasn't intruding. "I travel light," opined the lead guitarist who stood there smiling. He held a small overnight bag and he carried his guitar in a case.

That is where history stops on the magical summer night of June 12, 1970, and this is also where the story of what never was has its beginning. A week later, in the world we live in, Paul would announce that he was leaving the band, and suddenly the music fell silent. Guitars wept gently for what they could not say and for all that the future might otherwise offer from the Fab Four. But history is rarely true to what we know. For every event there exists a plethora of unrealized possibilities. It seems that the Argentine magic realist, Jorge Luis Borges, was correct in suggesting that time leads us along a garden path that forks away in a myriad of directions.

George Martin woke to a dream of music just before dawn on the morning of June 13, 1970. That is the time of day in the Caribbean when fog settles on the islands. Clouds cling to green hillsides and envelope rainforests in a semi-illumined shroud where everything is ancient and beyond time — time past, time present, and time yet to come. The music he heard was emanating from the garden path where the ground sloped toward the sea and blended with a gentle muffled sound of waves beating against the island. Fog hung in the boughs of the flamboyant trees as they opened their bright saffron lotus-shaped petals to the light embrace of mystery, the mystery that was about to unfold as a variant to the history we know. Martin stepped down from the porch and followed the path of sound. His first instinct inclined him to track the cobbles to the right, but in that fog on that particular day, he veered to the left and walked, almost stumbling through the mist. Drawn by a mystical force, he found himself arriving at where his Beatle guest sat upon a stone looking out into the impenetrable cloud-lost sea.

Harrison was strumming some chords and humming to himself. "I've been working on this since the last day in the studio when Paul blazed out and announced that it was over and John told him to fuck himself ... This is a song about something I learned in India." With that Harrison began to sing *All Things Must Pass*.

"You know, George," Harrison said, stopping and turning to Martin, "we need to cool off. We need to walk away but not for the last time." "How do you do that?"

"Tell the boys...you tell them because they won't listen to me...tell the boys to go away, work on their own pieces, their own things without the other three hanging about. If they want to bring one or two of us in, that'd be okay. But on their own. We were the sum of our parts. Isn't it a pity how we break each other's hearts? We'll do our own thing and then, in three years, we'll put it all together and see what we've got."

"Paul wants to do his own album."

Harrison laughed. "Yeah, well, let him. He's into livestock and heather these days. But if Paul thinks he's working on us, what remains of us, he'll give it his all."

"And then?"

"Then we just let it all fade away. We end on the right note, the chord that vanishes into a fog much like the one we're in."

By noon as the cloud burned off and as Harrison slept in the guest room, Martin made all the necessary calls. Glyn Johns said he was in. Paul was uncertain, but Martin told him to give it a go. Cool off. John sat silently on the other end of the trunk line as the phone sputtered and crackled across the Atlantic. Try as he might, nothing sarcastic came to his mind. Ringo simply said "why not?" That is how *The Cloud* album (1974) was born.

The cover depicts a single cloud misting in blue sky, large, billowed, and almost outsized, as if it were about to burst or simply drift away. It seemed as though it were the very cloud George Martin recalled having seen from the porch of that Anguilla house as the morning damp burned off to an acidic high noon above the Tropic of Cancer. There is no title lettering, neither on the front nor on the spine of the LP. On the back cover, a black and white photo depicts a path running down hill through a tropical garden in a dense fog, and the intention of the image is to make the viewer question where it would end, if ever, in the cloudy darkness of the overgrowth. It was as if the Beatles, for that moment the album spins on the turntable, existed and didn't exist. They were musicians who had outgrown their name; yet the unmistakeable sound of their voices immediately tells the listener that they are hearing John, Paul, George, and Ringo.

Inevitably, all the songs on *The Cloud* album, as it came to be known, would have been written anyway; but in the world where *The Cloud* album exists, the songs are brought together not merely because they are part of the product, but because they are offered up as each individual Beatle's best solo effort. The band that was the sum of all its parts finally proved that altogether now they were, without question, the greatest group of musicians the world will ever know.

Here is the play list from the two-disc album. You can read it on the back jacket. In the clear light of day, each Beatle decided to out-do the other. Even surreptitious projects that John and George worked on together in New York (with Paul's input on a song about the New York City subway system), made the mix – although even in the world where the garden path forked to the left, the grand hoax of Klaatu still lasted well beyond the lifetime of John Lennon. *The Cloud* album did not prevent John's assassination. That untimely death would have proven inevitable in any universe. Also, it did not stop the slow cancerous growth in George's brain, an enemy that eventually killed him decades later. All it did was to bring music to those who never wanted the miracle of the Beatles to end. And in the end, the love they made in the music was more than equal to anything they took with them.

Side One (Disc 1)

1 – What Is Life (Harrison)

2 – Instant Karma (Lennon)

3 – My Sweet Lord (Harrison)

4 – Working Class Hero (Lennon)

5 – Jet (McCartney)

6 – Band on the Run (McCartney)

7 – Whatever Gets You Through the Night (Lennon)

Side Two (Disc 1)

8 – If Not For You (Harrison)

9 – New York City (Lennon)

10 – Photograph (Starr)

11 – Calling Occupants (McCartney and Lennon)

12 – We're Off You Know (McCartney and Lennon)

13 – From a Window (McCartney and Lennon)

14 – World Without Love (Lennon and McCartney)

15 – Hey Bulldog (Lennon and McCartney)

Side Three (Disc 2)

16 – Maybe I'm Amazed (McCartney)

17 – Dear Christine (Lennon and McCartney)

18 – Give Me Love (Harrison)

19 – Watching the Wheels (Lennon)

20 – That Means a Lot (Lennon and McCartney)

21 – Nobody I Know (Lennon and McCartney)

22 – Subrosa (Lennon, McCartney, Harrison)

Side Four (Disc 2)

23 – That's the Way God Planned It (Preston and the Beatles)

24 – Something (Acoustic version) (Harrison)

25 – Calico Skies (McCartney)

26 – Yesterday (full band version) (Lennon and McCartney)

27 – Let It Be (single piano version) (McCartney)

28 – Imagine (Lennon)

29 – *All Things Must Pass* (Acoustic Anguilla version) (Harrison)

You can play this album for yourself. I have given you the map of songs it contains. I have set it up on my iPad as a playlist. The music in the night through tiny headphones goes with me on my travels. I listened to it last week as I lay in a hotel room in a city far away from home while lights from across the river flooded my room as if they were stars of a different universe. *The Cloud* album makes a strong statement about what could have been. I keep that statement of hope and love on both the tablet's memory, and also somewhere in the electronic stratosphere of the Apple cloud.

I close my eyes and picture that moment Martin took the mystical path straying to the left. In amazement he stands and listens to the sadness in Harrison's voice, a voice not yet grown old, a voice that clings tenaciously to a time when he was young. And with the last chords of George Harrison's personal Ecclesiastes on the nature of the world and friendships and the fading music of the soul that every ear longs to touch at some point in the noise and silence of the world, Martin walks back up the lawn to the porch of the house in Anguilla. Reaching the first step, he turns to look at what might have happened as he stares down the lawn into the fog where a variety of paths and a myriad of ways veer in their multitude of directions. And each one of those ways leads to a barely audible sea, as the most diaphanous of clouds touches the not-quite-visible trees and in the blush of a moment makes the leaves glisten.

Encountering Fame

John B. Lee

My son and I are standing on Bay Street
two feet from the curb
when the sirens sound
coming our way—a two-car escort
going importantly slow
their red lights swirling in sunlight
like perilous shallows of the rock-bound sea
and as they round the corner
where a woman stands like a mad prophet
wearing a home-spun Paul McCartney robe
the SUV arrives, the window eases down
and out leans the man himself
looking so much like himself it seemed
it might not be the *cute* Beatle
and for just a breath of a ten-breath moment
he crowded the gap in the dark glass
like a soft statue
that would not fit through time
something sacred
rocking on shoulders in a Sunday parade
and he waved
as it was in him to wave
and he looked our way
and my son—despite himself—shouted
"Paul" and fame looked and thengone
—that dog in a car
encounter—ended, and a girl
nearby—a sweet-sixteen girl
fainted—she eased her body
to the pavement
like an energetic deflation
and she lay there smiling

and her father and sister knelt
gave comforting
supplication to unconscious beauty
and my heart pounded
like a child trapped in a travel trunk
marked 1964

Dirás que soy un soñador pero no soy el unico ...

John B. Lee

As my uncle lay dying in palliative care, a harried nurse too busy to attend to her every trust in a timely fashion gave my cousin Susan and I a task we would prove we were not up to. The poor man had been unable to take solid food for nearly three full days, and he lay in a fitful state of near consciousness, feckless and malnourished, his body cloaked in a single white sheet tossed over his thinning frame like something thrown over statuary in a midnight museum, his hands thereby trapped in linen, his visible tongue coated the purple white of candlewax.

Our job involved holding a translucent green oxygen mask over his mouth and nose so that the moisture in the breathing machine might give comfort to his shallow inhalations. Cousin Susan snapped the elastic bands in place behind his ears and held the mask firmly so it made an airtight seal along his face from cheekbone to chin. Satisfied that it was properly set, she released her grip on the breathing device. Uncle John's right hand struggled to release itself from bondage and inched its way up to his jawline, thereby shakily removing the mask. Cousin Susan, all the while reassuring him that this was her duty, and that he would gain comfort in breathing, insisted the green mask back into place, setting my uncle's quivering hand aside as though he were a misbehaving and thankless child.

"It's alright Uncle John," I added in an effort to reassure him that this was necessary. We were, after all, his loving kin. I was slightly surprised by the lack of moisture appearing on the inner dome of the mask. Hadn't I seen it damp and bedewed and fogged with working when the nurse had placed it over his mouth and nose? Why was there no evidence to confirm his shallow suppuration? Perhaps his breathing was even shallower than I had thought. Again, his hands struggled with the sheet, his strength tested by the weight of seams, as though he were weak and pale as cool light lifting through thin fog. Again, he managed to reach his chin with his quivering fingers. Again he willfully removed the mask, as though he would defy the very gods with this late-life recalcitrance. "I'll do as I wish. I'll do what I damned well please!" This was my uncle, defiant to the end.

Showing great kindness, her patience and tolerance tested to the limit, cousin Susan replaced the mask and held it firmly over his mouth and nose, reassuring her beloved bachelor uncle with every cell in her body, mustering the strength in her deep resolve to do the task to which she had been appointed. Uncle John's frail hand struggled for release. She stood her ground, insisting the necessity of that damned mask she held in place as though it were a small pillow and she were smothering a king.

At that moment the nurse returned to see how things were coming along, and she almost shrieked, "What are you doing?" as she flipped a switch and the machine feeding oxygen and moisture to the mask came to life. We had inadvertently starved him of oxygen, all the while thinking we were boosting his breathing, we had been smothering him, euthanizing our uncle, reassuring him as he struggled for breath we had been sending him to a better world.

This was the very same uncle who had lifted me high on his shoulders when I was a lad, swung me into place so I rode his body striding beneath door frames like a big horse in a small barn. This was the very same Uncle who had introduced me to the Beatles almost fifty years ago on that winter night in 1964. This was the very man who had kindly said, "You stay there and listen to that," leaving me in the farm truck with the radio tuned to CFCO in Chatham, playing "A Day in the Life." This dying man at whose bedside I sat vigil only months ago as he slipped from this world like ice from warmth on glass, who'd said he'd lost his faith in God the night he'd sent the empty coffin of a friend into the chill waters of the north Atlantic during the last great war.

It seems we learn as we live. Lessons await our attention every moment of every day. A few years prior to his death in his ninetieth year, I had been in Cuba, and not thinking of him at all. My wife Cathy and I were standing in the Vedado district of Havana, on the sidewalk just outside of the park on the corner of 17th and 6th street, visiting the statue of John Lennon immortalized in bronze unveiled on December 8th, 2000 on the twentieth anniversary of his assassination outside the gates of his gothic residence at the Dakota, near Central Park, Manhattan, New York City.

Fidel Castro had had a change of heart concerning this particular Beatle. Quoting Lennon's song, Imagine, he had said, "Dirás que soy un soñador, pero no soy el unico ..." essentially saying, "I too am a dreamer." On the twentieth anniversary of Lennon's murder, the statue was unveiled. The original statue included a pair of John Lennon wire-rim spectacles sans lenses. Unfortunately, visitors stole the glasses so often that it became necessary to post as guard, an old man, who for a single convertible peso would restore the glasses to the nose of the bronze likeness of Mr. Lennon so that the tourists might take a photograph of themselves sitting park bench next to Winston O' Boogie. Cathy and I enjoyed our brief visit and then headed off for the Colon Cemetery, one of the most famous of all cemeteries in the Caribbean. We were standing on a street corner consulting a map when a middle age Cuban dressed in an ice-suit tapped me on the shoulder, and in perfect English offered to assist us.

When he learned where we had been and where we were going, he said, "It's on my way home, I'll walk along with you for a while if I may, and I'll show you the way." He asked me if I liked the Beatles, and when we confirmed a mutual admiration for the music of the fab four, he offered up the following story.

"When I was a teenager," he said, "The Beatles were banned in Cuba along with all other American music. But one of my friends managed to get a copy of their single, 'From Me to You,' and since I had a record player, we used to gather at my house to listen to that record. One day when we got carried away with our enthusiasm for the music, dancing in my house and playing the record dangerously loud, the informer who lived on the corner of our street reported us to the police. The Beatles were contraband, counterrevolutionary music, you understand. If you were caught with one of their records you could be arrested. At the very least, the police would seize and destroy the record. When the police came knocking at my door, we barely heard their loud rapping over the music. Eventually, I heard the commotion and immediately turned off the record player and answered the door. There stood a young police officer demanding that I surrender the record and the record player. He stated that I was in possession of prohibited American music. I was a brazen youth, so the first thing I said to him was that the record we had been listening to was not American, but British. The Beatles are British I said, as if that were anything like a persuasive argument. I noticed that he was young, and so I added, come into my house and listen to this record with us. If you do not like the music, then you may have the record and I will go with you. The police officer reluctantly complied with my request. As he listened a smile crept over his face. He agreed that the music was magical. He told me in future to be more careful not to be overheard by the neighbours. And he left, and my friends and I had many years of pleasure listening to that forbidden music."

At that moment, just as he finished his story, we arrived at the corner of his street. He pointed to the house occupying the corner lot and said indignantly, "That is where the informer lived."

"Does he still live there?" I asked.

"No." he replied. "One day the police came and took him away."

"What happened to him?"

"I don't care," he said. And so he walked on down the street to his home and Cathy and I proceeded from there, with this story of a time in Cuba before the recent period of ideological revisionism. The memory of John Lennon lives on, not only in John Lennon Park in Havana. In a resort in Guradalavaca, there stands another statue struck in the likeness of John Lennon circa 1968. And in Holguín, second largest city in Cuba, there is a club called La Caverna, with bronze statues of all four of the Beatles. My friend Wency Rosales took me there for a drink and I happily had my photograph taken with a likeness of young John Lennon.

A few years ago, at Abbey of Gethsemani, a Trappist monastery in Kentucky, I met a Russian singer songwriter named Misha Feigin. We began chatting about poetry and music. He is a highly respected guitarist who has performed for the president of the United States. Very early in our conversation I inquired about the quality of his English and he confirmed, that like almost every Russian of his generation, he'd learned English listening to Beatle records. In the film, Paul McCartney in Red Square, one middle-age historian opined, "Credit for the collapse of the Soviet Union has more to do with a generation of young people listening to Beatle records than it has to do with Ronald Reagan, Mikhail Gorbachev, and Glasnost. Glasnost is a direct result of the liberating influence of the Beatles." Misha is a poet for whom the Beatles remain a major influence. In his poem, "An Old Record," he reveals the impact of that early influence.

An Old Record

Misha Feigin

Suddenly, it is back –
A vague wave of sound
Clouds all good things
In my room I think I knew,
Long lost longing,
The blood thinks again...

Music never leaves the atmosphere,
Only waits to be triggered,
But where is the root
Of this urge?

I think it is in the bones,
And in the skin,
And in the muscles,
And in the internal organs -
The same place
Where the strength to stop
It lives.

Only a few days ago, on a trip to China, I sat in the bus on our way to visit Tiananmen Square, that famous mall located just outside the gate to the Forbidden City. At one end of the square a large movie screen broadcasting colourful advertisements for the latest commodities reminds one of the big screen over Times Square in Manhattan. At the other end of the square, a large picture of Chairman Moa reminds this traveler of the Yangju incident when a young Chinese dissident walking the white line of Chang'an Avenue stood in the path of a stream of tanks sent into the heart of the city to repress the student uprising. Our guide, a thirty-eight year old Chinese man spoke with disgust for the 'largest museum in the world' containing nothing but Red Art of no interest from the period of the Cultural Revolution. His own father, a party member, had been arrested and without trial been 're-educated' and required to do forced labour in the reconstruction of the Great Wall. Between the time of his arrest and the time of his return, he lost over one hundred and fifty pounds. When he came home, his own wife did not recognize him.

Our guide, with the self-chosen easily pronounceable Anglo name, Frank Lee, spoke of how he had grown up in the country amusing himself by dripping wax on the wings of a pet cricket in order to change the pitch and tone of his song. He spoke of learning English listening to forbidden Beatle music. He had managed to acquire two audiotapes. The official response to contraband Beatle music involved the seizing of all banned tapes and records. If a guard discovered a banned tape, he was instructed to shoot it with a nail gun. According to Frank, one guard adjusted the nail gun so the nail, intended for the tape's destruction, would penetrate the case without destroying the tape. Frank had managed to acquire two nearly playable tapes. He had a copy of "Yellow Submarine," and a copy of "One," the latter being a late release of Beatle singles that had gone to number one on the charts in America. Frank said, "I nursed the tape from the smashed case, and painstakingly inserted in into a new case. If the tape was damaged, I very carefully scotch taped it together at the broken point. That is how I first learned English," he said proudly. "I learned English because I loved the music of the Beatles."

Early one morning on the farm, I sat on the el of the front veranda singing like a songbird hidden in the branches of a maple tree. I'd thought I was alone. I sang, "Yesterday, all my troubles seemed so far away ..." My Uncle John caught me there and inquired with a smirk in his voice, "What the hell are you doing?"

"I'm singing," I said. I might have said, were it only a few years later, "you may say I'm a dreamer, but I'm not the only one ..." And I almost think he might have understood, though he certainly would never have sung along.

Beatle Dreams

for son, David, John, Rob and Colin, the Paper Lions.

Hugh MacDonald

Oft likened to invading Beatles,
who landed laughing, 1964*,
(that much more innocent, happy year),
our young Paper Lions, inhabit a world
too rich in music no one pays for,
—this fresh four from tiny PEI
who'll never set foot in Liverpool,
never play the Casbah Coffee Club,
nor tip a pint of ale at Ye Crack,
yet have rocked China, rolled the North Pole,
and oft spanned their home and native land—
yet stand poised to thrill the U.S.A.,
to court America with their songs
YouTubed around the globe to millions,
driving Maine to California,
rocking, raunchy songs, sweet harmonies,
fan base growing fatter note by note,
feeling on the verge of something big,
their music, their dreams, never ending.
Alive and hope-filled, driving onward,
all tracks they leave uplift adoring hearts.

**Reference to the Beatles Landed Laughing in New York, John B. Lee, BMP, 1995.*

The Beatles at the Edgewater

Susan Evans Shaw

Edgewater Inn, a place where the Beatles once stayed. Just to ensure guests recognized the hotel's claim to fame, the management had a large photo of them "fishing" from the window of their suite posted at the reception desk.

In 1994 the Geological Society of America was meeting in Seattle. My husband had filled in the conference accommodation form. A mid-price hotel on the waterfront seemed an attractive choice. Unaware of the hotel's celebrity, we found ourselves in what seemed a remote part of the city far from the conference centre. Anticipating a lively reunion with friends seen only at these gatherings, I felt exiled to no-man's-land.

August 21, 1964, the Beatles spent a night here. Edgewater was the only hotel in Seattle that would take the risk of having them as guests. Fears of riots and damage made the Fab Four unwelcome at all the respectable downtown hotels. The solitary Edgewater, built on a pier as part of an unrealized waterfront development, desperately needed a boost or it was in danger of being shut down. Manager Don Wright decided to take a chance. He arranged for barricades of plywood and barbed wire to be erected. Three days insurance at exorbitant rates had to be paid and the hotel braced for a siege.

The Beatles arrived by limousine, pulling up at the entrance amid the screams of fans from outside the barricade. Suite 272, with an exceptional view over Elliott Bay, was the very best the Edgewater had to offer. There the Beatles remained, leaving only for their performance at the Seattle Coliseum, imprisoned by an adoring mob. Posing for publicity photos by fishing from the suite window made for a diversion. No mention of any fish caught. Next morning after breakfast they left for the airport.

Immediately the four were gone, Suite 272 was stripped. The carpet was taken up and cut into squares to be sold as souvenirs. The sheets, beds, lamps and furniture were distributed among other suites in the hotel to prevent future guests from stealing mementos. With hotel property thus protected, the manager began to spread the word of the illustrious visitors. The hotel has prospered to the present day.

Our ground floor room faced over the water. Otherwise it was unmemorable, a hotel room like many another—a bed, a dresser, a mini bar, television and a bathroom with all the fittings—until I looked down from the window. Dark and dirty water lapped at the foundations a few feet directly below me. The bay was calm, just the slow hypnotic back and forth of tidal water on the move. A sign posted on the sill: "No fishing from hotel windows."

Unlike the Beatles, we were free to come and go. We set out in search of the conference centre. On the landward side, the district surrounding the hotel looked flat and vacant. To me the area resembled Hamilton's abandoned CNR yard. A tram traveled back and forth on its rails as regularly as the waves under our window. A broad boulevard, a few trees dotted along its length and the occasional passing car— not a very busy place at that time of day.

Above the waterfront, buildings perched on the edge of an escarpment. Signs pointed across the tracks to a walkway leading to what looked like an oversized iron fire escape. Up we climbed to a sort of vestibule and a door through which we passed into another world—brilliantly lit, noisy, smelly, Pike Place Market, crammed with stalls displaying fruits, vegetables, fish, souvenirs; aisles crowded by shoppers and tourists.

We left the market, exiting onto Pike Street. Down-and-out natives populated the square outside the gaudy market entrance, some begging, some just loitering, smoking cigarette ends and drinking from paper cups. Most looked hungry and unwashed. We passed by. There were too many even to consider offering a coin or two. They eyed us with indifference. Just a block further on we joined the bustling, prosperous crowds of shoppers and business people.

John, Paul, George and Ringo came from Liverpool; each with family links to that northern industrial port. In 1964, in a hotel room overlooking the water, they were not that far removed from their origins.

Encore ...

The book ***Window Fishing: the night we caught Beatlemania****, edited by Poet Laureate John B. Lee, certainly captures the total early 60s excitement of those adventurous and novel times ... the nonplussedness of the parents' generation and the dedicated headlong drive into Beatledom of the younger teenagers ... No-one knew where this was leading ... and maybe we still don't know ... but youngsters were electrified into exhilarating life at the sound of a few bars of music. Or the oh-so-simple count of, 'one, two, three, four' ... We all knew what was coming next! All round the world, we suddenly became members of the same club ... a club which included the older generation as had never been before ... and the belonging badge of honour had on it four distinctive haircuts on four distinctive faces. Welcome to Beatlemania.*

Julia Baird,
sister of Beatle John Lennon

Leaving Liverpool 1961

Frances Roberts-Reilly

From Birkenhead to Scouse land, the ferry churns the Mersey; them Liver birds squawking. Adorned in bright blue glitter eye shadow, peroxided hair, screaming vulgarities about last night's shag above the wind. "It's a dirty story of a dirty man."

"Beneath the blue suburban skies", dreary rows of monochrome council houses. Boys form packs on bikes weaving along sidewalks: 'Ang on a mo. Ooh she 'ad it off. Delivering a knuckle sandwich to anyone who dares commit agro. Circling around

The docks, the back alleys, the old warehouses; slave trade shame and point of embarkation of the Irish weary of misery. Dreams abandoned and left behind, others fail on unfriendly shores, yet more are sacrificed for $1 an hour wage. No future there. "Ah look at all the lonely people, where do they all belong?" Above the throng, a lament

"Nowhere Man, are you listening?" Now sniffing the air for a whiff of a chip butty that's not fab enough for a posh twat, "Protected by a silver spoon." None of it, this life makes the news unless "she's the kind of girl who makes The News of the World." Cos the only way out is for a girl is "Got to be good looking." That's how a girl can "See how the other half lives." Squinting, trying desperately to

Focus on something real. Shurrup you! The boys have their soccer, but what's a girl to do? "Nothing is real. Nothing to get hung up about." Now clenching fists, "One two three four five six seven, All good children go to Heaven."

Willing the word to come alive; "Say the word I'm thinking. Have you heard the word is love?" A ghost of reassurance floats past; "Don't you know it's gonna be alright."

How come leaving is so hard? So many came and went with the tide. Too many wasted lives. Yeah, dream on why don't ya? Betraying the

Horlick's happy family dream, "She's leaving home, after living alone, for so many years." She stands at the corner of Hope Street, looks out over the water. "Yes, I'm gonna be a star."

Note: I spent my early teen years wondering how to get out of England. I was bright and industrious, but lacking the advantage of an education to get me out of my working class destiny. In England, The Beatles through grit and talent were able to break through the class system barriers and leave the working class behind. This opened a floodgate for the rest of us. The Beatles' performance on the Ed Sullivan Show in 1964 marked a clarion call to those of us with so much potential to finally realize our dreams. I arrived in Canada in 1968.

In writing the poem I went through the lyrics of many Beatles songs and found a thread of meaning that spoke directly to the disillusionment and alienation of youth. Particularly, young women like myself who had nothing left to lose by leaving a suffocating and bleak future. These refrains are embedded in the poem along with some Scouse slang in common usage by Liverpool natives that augment the poet's narrative. I was 16 years old in 1961.

Not from farms and freshwater lakes

Kathleen Abley

i tell you
there is salt in me
so many times
have i looked back
and again   one last look
for who am i without a past
my memory and storytell
so if i stiffen solid
as salt lick   as lot's wife did
then someone savor me

comb me layer by layer
from summer salt sea
the shallow seaside ponds
when winds blow in just right
where salt
hand harvested
was worth its weight in gold
a salary paid
in crystal   coarse and grey
from celtic seas

carve a chapel where i stand
let the wind to me
or set me to the sea
ocean brine will be my curing
as I look back
to ancestors
with blood of viking
and of celt
stevedores   sailors   seamen
fish-market women   working
rearing children   cooking
all knew the worth of salt

The Cavern Club

Kimmy Beach

I cross over Mathew Street
through the ten-at-night stick of sweating locals
tourists   low-cut tops and high high heels
drizzled damp and echo on a hundred wooden stairs
curling   descending into The Cavern Club
(a fake Cavern   the original
up the street bulldozed
a shopping centre, underground train,
two cafés in its place)

in this replica cave
a fake Beatles band under stone
bounces "Please Please Me" off thick wet walls
dancing bodies   pumping speakers
the Paul is right-handed
he doesn't look at all like you

condensation   sweat   love
drip on me from the rounded ceiling
turn my face to it
moisture runs down my neck
soaks into my collar
the band shakes the room
the stage pounding
my wineglass on the speaker
vibrates toward the edge with each
kick of the bass drum
a ripple of wine spiraling from the centre

a man in a long leather coat
takes my picture from behind a stone arch
his pint of Fosters on a small shelf at his elbow
he moves to dance behind me   his chin at my shoulder
his breath moves my hair

we dance at the side of the stage
walls rattle
noise and stink of too many people
too much ale
music too loud
I am so high

so deep

underground

The Beatles

Laurence Hutchman

With a burst of energy
their music shimmered
on The Ed Sullivan Show.
We grew our hair long,
we danced
until the songs became
our personal and universal videos.

That summer night riding the freight train
from Jasper to Edmonton,
standing on the oil platform
I was singing, "It's been a hard day's night"

In Paris at *Le Bar Americain*
as I struggled to speak
in broken high school French to girls
the words find me
"Michelle, ma belle
Sonts les mots . . . très bien ensemble."

We all were living with the Beatles
in a yellow submarine,
in the sky with the psychedelic Lucy
and on "Strawberry Fields Forever."

Give me back

Roger Bell

Give me back fifty years.
Give me mini-skirted thighs and lewd longings
and Sunday nights of Ed and awe
and hair down over distrustful eyes
and insolence,
and invasion.

Give me back fifty years
and all the energy that lies therein-
and I will again put possibility onto the turntable,
drop the stylus into its spiral inward groove
and spin the world that will be,
dizzy with our dreaming.

When you're 64

Betsy Struthers

So, there's comfort to be found on a night like this,
first barbecue of the season and the sun not set
at ten to eight. Say, an hour ago, we were listening
to the Countdown on Radio 2 and what plays
is Daft Punk's "Get Lucky." Okay, they're
not the Beatles and this is definitely not
the 60s. Still, I love you, yeah
yeah, yeah.

Night, She Says

Roy Bentley

The yellow-skirted babysitter does a lewd shimmy,
slide-stepping to the fridge for a Coca-Cola. She's
a German major at UD, is hip to John Paul George
and Ringo, and brings her own phonograph records,

33s, to stack on my father's turntable, introducing me
to *Introducing the Beatles*, hand-carried from Hamburg,
and all this before Ed Sullivan hands them over
like an instance of beauty made double in the right light.

She's got on fishnets; and when there's no music,
none that I can hear yet, at 10, clasps my left hand
and we faux-tango off to my bed beneath the Crucifix.
Thank you, Jesus, I whisper. "Night," she says.

In the morning I flex my pecs and biceps, recalling
the spontaneous choreography of Wanda Goff.
Mother says, "What's gotten into you, mister?"
But my father, who drove Wanda home, tucks in

his tank top; he smiles, all forearms and swelling chest.
Then yellow light streams in through the one long
kitchen window, and I know why it takes breath
to fill a body the rest of the way, why fish-net stockings

make blood rush down the concourse of affirmation.
When I'm too old to twist and shout, too lively yet
to die, I pray for a Beatles tune, any, and a dancer
easy with the bump and grind of self, who shimmies.

A Day in the Life

Roy Bentley

Consider it: to break out a twelve-string pawnshop guitar
and launch into an original song in 1972 must have required
not just confidence. The smooth spun steel of those strings
in rough hands fashioning makeshift chords for the reason
you want—need—to hear exhortations of your own making.
The shellacked shine of the guitar body, the bruised wood
vibrating, then the vocals and arpeggios—what audacity

to risk everything in some new friend's basement room.
So what if The Beatles sing "A Day in the Life". Lennon
and McCartney started somewhere. Nets of fantasy haul in
their catch of fish from the dim few cubic feet of Ohio air.
Shoulder-length hair mimes the wingbeats of shore birds
crossing a whitecapped lake of Now. Hard not to applaud
one who scours a Burger King to the point of spotlessness

for shit wages then croons so hopefully of made-up places.
There's a break for a Marlboro, the hammers of addiction
tapping out blood rhythms as smoke seethes and flutters.
Someone shouts *Keep it down!* The work seems endless.
Like draining exhausted grease from fryers, disentangling
logistical trials in the small-town wee hours of third shift.
Like shooting black-pajamed VC after VC in the head

or in the region of a beating heart must have to others.
Gone are the days of knights in armor. King Arthur
would sit at a table of round and Robin Hood fought
for the poor... You're starting in again. Same tune
but with summer storms accompanying, a hard rain
recalling what Bob Dylan said about there being no
success like failure. That failure is no success at all.

I thought I knew you, what did I know

Mark Tovey

I once had the habit of thinking
of my friends in terms of
music they reminded me of.
This one, *Rubber Soul*, that one
Sgt. Pepper's Lonely Hearts Club Band.
For me, the music, in its
association, seemed neatly to
encapsulate their personalities.

Once in a fit of self-revelation
I told someone how I thought
their wonderfulness could be
summed up by a record.

Perhaps I didn't say it right.

Anyway, I don't think of people that way
any more.

Someone get me outta here

Mark Tovey

I've watched him raise his camera
and take pictures of a throng of people
who were photographing him.

Unless Paul uses his SLR as a prop,
he must have astonishing photos of people
with cameras at the ready.

A gallery filled with those photos
would convey the overwhelm
a Beatle must daily contend with.

An SLR has an added virtue.
When held in front of the face,
one is completely hidden from view.

Some people have photographs of Paul,
with face obscured, taking a picture of them -
Not the photo they wanted.

It seems fair turnabout.
If people are photographing you,
you should be able to photograph them.

A useful intervention for celebrities
who wish to evade the photographic crush
with grace.

The Handshake

Mark Tovey

On November 19th, 1997, a group of friends and I had gone to Carnegie Hall to hear Paul McCartney's then-new orchestral piece, *Standing Stone*. We also had tickets for Paul McCartney's appearance the very next morning on the *Oprah Winfrey Show.* In order to get good seats, however, it was necessary to line up hours ahead of time.

When I arrived in the middle of the night to line up, there was no one else there. Actually, there was one other person there. That person was asleep on the sidewalk, oblivious to my presence. I strongly suspected that he wasn't actually there to watch Paul McCartney perform on the Oprah Winfrey show.

Gradually a line began to form, and one by one my friends joined me. At one point people from the Oprah show came and gave everyone in line hot chocolate. Security was tight. We were searched before entering. They let me keep a CD which I had brought along to give to Paul if I got a chance. The CD featured a classical piece by Leoš Janáček, which sounded a bit like McCartney's piano composition, "A Leaf". The orchestral version of "A Leaf" had been played at Carnegie Hall the night before, and had been well received highlights of the concert at Carnegie Hall.

Before either Oprah or Paul entered, the producers came in and rehearsed the crowd in cheering. The producers were quite serious about elevating the level of our cheers so that the energy was at a fever pitch when Paul came in. They kept asking us to get louder. However our rehearsal didn't prepare anyone for how the roof was blown off the place when Paul finally entered, calm and relaxed. I was told afterwards that he received the biggest cheer they had ever had on the show.

Waiting all night had its advantages. We managed to get seats in the front row, at the same level as the stage. Paul occupied the chair directly facing us. The fact that we were sitting within easy conversational distance gave us the opportunity to chitchat with Paul during the commercial breaks. In one case, the crew came in to dab his face, probably to remove the beads of perspiration that built up under the hot lights. The breaks were short. Long answers weren't possible, but if you were quick, you could get a brief answer to a specific question while the crew busied themselves. I asked Paul, for instance, whether he was working on new classical music—"Oh, oh yes... definitely!".

After Oprah finished her interview, the audience was given an opportunity to ask Paul questions. To my delight, Paul pointed at me to ask the last question.

I had mentally rehearsed my question several times, to make sure I got it right: "We were all charmed by the orchestral version of "A Leaf" at last night's *Standing Stone*. How did you write the original piece, and what was involved in putting together the orchestral version?"

Paul gave a lengthy answer. The gist of Paul's response was: "I brought in Jonathan Tunick, and we did an arrangement." Rather than directing his answer to Oprah, he spoke directly to me. When Paul gives you his attention, it is his entire attention. I had a chance to speak with other people who had asked him questions, and they had the same experience.

After the interview portion ended, Paul played songs from his then new release, *Flaming Pie*. This was an album which marked the beginning of what I like to call the McCartney renaissance, seemingly spurred on by the *Beatles Anthology* and his newfound willingness to reclaim his past.

In a hundred years we may only remember the Beatles catalogue, or we may make little distinction between the work of the Fabs together and their best solo work. Or we may pick certain periods to cherish. If so, this will be one of them.

As the show ended, the audience cheered, one final long cheer. I noticed a couple of people going up to shake his hand, so I followed suit. I had expected a bassist's handshake—beefy somehow—instead I encountered long, thin fingers, almost delicate—a painter's hands.

An almost perfect day. I have only one regret. I didn't reach for the CD I had brought to give him. So, Paul, if you happen to be reading this, you might want to check out Janáček's "On the Overgrown Path". You'll be glad you did.

I've seen Sir Paul McCartney in concert five times, and as of July 7th I'll be traveling to Pittsburg to see him a sixth. The first time I saw him I sat so far from the stage that he shrank down in the distance from my vantage point to the size of Gulliver's nemesis Lilliputian Emperor Mully Ully Gue. From that far away I could have blanked the entire pipsqueak of his body to invisibility by simply holding up my thumb. Seated in the last row of the upper tier of the closed roof of the Sky Dome, I reached overhead and touched the inner skin of the grey ceiling with the palm of my hand before I sat down in the shivering dizzy vertigo where the air thins from altitude.

On another occasion in Toronto at the Air Canada Centre, I was thrilled by the drone of my hometown Port Dover marching band heralding their entrance with the tattoo of the drums and the skirling of the pipes played to the haunting strains of Paul singing "Mull of Kintyre."

In New York City, my son and I sat on third base line of the ball diamond a hundred yards from the man himself. We could almost smell the sweat silkening his shirt in the summer heat. The shock of the powder blast pushed the pyrotechnics of "Live and Let Die" so hard we felt the whoosh of heat and noise enough to sting our nostrils and stun our ears.

In Kanata, near Ottawa, we sat on the cement stairs leading to the entrance gate of our section and ensconced there we heard the entire sound check with the local police pipe band as they practiced and practiced again Paul's anthem from the Mull. If Paul McCartney remains an apotheosis of sorts because of the quality of his voice, the beauty of his songs, the virtuosity of his playing, and the energy of his music, then seeing Ringo is certainly the most fun I've ever had at a concert.

I saw him first in Orillia, then in Niagara Falls Canada. And truth be told, he's a joyful crowd pleaser. From the days when he was America's favourite Beatle, he has always been a source of jubilation and plain ordinary good fun. In the early sixties when he shook his hair the crowd went wild. Now, when he enters the venue and shouts his question "What's my name?" the entire audience responds with a chorus of joyful noise in a surging of one voice "Ringo."

The next time I saw him, my son and I sat in the second row. As is my habit, I cross my arms and listen. I'm not one for singing along, or stamping my feet, or clapping my hands out of time. I'm inclined to sit very still, keeping my joy close to my heart. And thus, inadvertently I caught Ringo's attention. He was singing into a hand-held microphone, standing on his mark downstage centre, when my presence caught his eye. He looked my way, tucked the microphone under his arm, pointing in my direction, crossed his arms thus mirroring my posture, he shrugged seeming to say "enjoy yourself, lad, loosen up" and then he resumed his vocal leaving me laughing and relaxed and thinking to myself, "I've had Ringo's attention! Ringo Starr of the Beatles plucked me out of the crowd even if only for a fleeting moment. My life is now complete."

Of course, I'd already been the object of Paul's delight. I'd been standing on the curb when he drove past, leaned out from the window of his limo, pointed my way and shouted a greeting.

I've tried that story out twice. The first time I told friend Bruce Meyer that tale, he told me he'd almost been struck by Paul McCartney's car in London. McCartney rolled his window down, leaned out and said to him, "Are you alright mate?" The second time I told the story, the fellow whom I told, a guy named Mark Tovey, revealed that he had shaken McCartney's hand on Oprah Winfrey's talk show. He'd been invited there as a special guest of the staff. He'd asked McCartney the final question of the day. And then, he'd been invited down to stage after the show for a meet and greet. And Sir Paul had shaken his hand. "He has the most delicate fingers I've ever felt," said Mark. "Musician's hands," he added.

Perhaps I'll never tell the story of my encounter with Paul again (though I write it here). I'll hold it close and cherish my own special moment with Beatle Paul looking so much like himself he could have been himself. As for Ringo, I'll be seeing him again in June, in Orillia. Or better yet, he'll be seeing me. I wonder if he'll remember me. I doubt it, but I'll be keeping my arms crossed just in case.

John B. Lee

Ringo Starr Answers Questions On Larry King Live About The Death Of George Harrison

Roy Bentley

First, Larry King mistakenly calls Ringo
George then asks him whether his passing,
George's, was expected. He answers that it was.
Says they knew he was sick. Had lung cancer.
I'm watching, though it's none of my business
how grief-stricken Ringo Starr was and likely
still is or whether he was there, at the bedside,
at the moment George left his life for some other,
if you can believe what George believed, which
was that we keep coming back till we get it right.
And when Ringo is about to let down his guard
and be a bit more self-disclosing, even honest,
Larry interrupts, asking, Do you ever want to
pinch yourself? And Ringo Starr says, Sure.
In 1988, years before, in another interview,
with George, this years after Lennon's death,
Ringo confessed that he was the poorest Beatle
then laughed and blew cigarette smoke upward.
Which must've seemed terribly funny to George,
an inside joke, because he said Hello, John to
the smoke like it was Lennon (by virtue of his
acknowledged wealth) or some spirit he used to
conquer worlds with. Ringo says he was shocked
upon hearing the news of the death of John Lennon,
but that George's death was another thing entirely.
He doesn't quote from the Bhagavad Gita, but it's
as if he wants to say we continue on, are these spirits,
a sort of outrageous bliss even to think it, dumb luck
on the order of being hired as the Beatles' drummer.
Maybe he would have said it, with respect to George
or ventured his own beliefs, if Larry hadn't butted in

to ask him which of the Beatles was the best musician.
You mean, now? And I want to laugh now because
maybe Ringo's imagining how hard it is to move
your hands after you're dead, or to move at all,
and how impossible it must be to keep time
and tempo in all that anonymous blankness,
the dark become your most imploring fan.

November 30th, 2001 only a day after the untimely death of George Harrison, a momentous year of lies and promises, only one day short of a week since my 50th birthday then, the Friday of the public waking of the shy Beatle at the Strawberry Fields Memorial in Central Park, New York City, and I was there. My wife and I had taken a bus to the city, and then a water taxi past the smouldering remains of American hope. The remnants of disaster draped in plastic that rattled tall sheeting in the chill wind drifting in off the Hudson. It singed our lungs to breathe that smouldering grief. The captain of our vessel spoke of how they'd abandoned all tourists and rescued people from the five points, their faces choked, and their nostrils black with chemical soot. We rounded the point at Battery Park passing the noisome garbage scows busy in the come and go of trash trolling shadow under the Brooklyn Bridge. We made our pilgrimage, later strolling past the Dakota Apartments, the gothic residence of the famous widow and her fatherless son. I walked to the bloodstained place where Lennon fell. I stood there in the spectral silence, and though I did not weep, I mourned. I thought of life and death and the thin thread of fate that sometimes fails to hold us here. And from there we meandered through gates of the park, and headed down the path to follow the sound of the music coming as though from the earth. There were dozens of sad troubadours singing Harrison songs. There were those who could barely play, and those who sang in reedy voices thin as bone. There were caterwauls and sweet surmises, girls with candles held and barely flickering against the breath of weather in the light. I had not come for this, but luck was mine and I was there the day they waked the youngest of the four young lads from Liverpool. I stayed and thought of him, the one with the sore throat, the one with the fever, the one who performed a little shuffle dance and smiled to play his red guitar the night they came to shake the world. And he was only twenty-one. The manager called them 'the boys,' and that was true. And if I say, the makers and the spoilers seem to rule the world, his was a maker's time and he a man who gave his youth away and smiled to gift us with his songs.

John B. Lee

The Day We (Sort Of) Met George Harrison

Chris Faiers

It was late summer. A bunch of L'Auberge regulars decided to take a Sunday trek to see George Harrison, who was rumoured to be living in a little village named Esher. We hopped on the double-decker bus in Richmond, and after an hour or so of riding we arrived in Esher. The ten of us were a scraggly lot, all would-be hippies trying to grow our hair long, the girls dressed in shawls and long skirts and granny boots.

Our goals were the standard ones in 1969 - California Jon, Canadian Peter and a couple of other guitarists had made a tape, and wanted Harrison's opinion of it. I had a copy of my just printed haiku chapbook, Cricket Formations, and I hoped to get up enough nerve to present my poems to my idol. And of course we all wanted to meet a real live Beatle!

Harrison was my favourite Beatle, largely because he was the one closest to me in physical appearance, with his craggy face and dark hair. I had modeled my haircut and clothes on Harrison for some time. I also thought he was the most interesting Beatle because of his enthusiasm for Eastern mysticism.

Someone had gotten good directions, for we actually found Harrison's house without a lot of trouble. Located in a very staid, upper-middle-class suburban neighbourhood, the house stood out like a psychedelic advertisement. A high fence bordered the large lot, and the house was painted a myriad of colours, like something out of the movie Yellow Submarine. We were all entranced to be setting foot in a sacred preserve of Beatledom, and after knocking on the door and receiving no answer, we boldly began surveying the premises.

"MICK & MARIANNE WUZ HERE!" was spray painted on the front wall, and this further consecrated the property. Our rock heroes actually lived here, visited with each other, slept together, and had probably done these wild paintings on acid trips like our own. We were all strengthened in our faith as true believers in hippiedom.

Some of the group camped by the front door, and the guitar payers started scratching on their ubiquitous instruments. I wandered around, and found a pair of George's jeans hanging on a clothesline. For a fleeting moment I was tempted to steal them, to see if my hero's jeans would fit.

Manicured lawn
would-be hippies wait
for a Beatle

A touch of the Beatles' famous ironic humour was present in a large wooden cross leaning against the back fence. I even had the nerve to peek in the draped windows. On the window ledge of one room was a collection of seashells. Miracle of miracles - there was even an apple tree - how appropriate for the founders of Apple records. If there was a heaven on earth, this was it for Beatle fans.

Seashell lined window
apples rotting in the yard
suburban fences

I rejoined the group on the front lawn, and soon a mini-car came scooting up the drive, quickly followed by a luxury sedan. The driver of the mini got out, and a not-very-pleased looking George Martin confronted us. He wanted to know what we were doing, and while we all sat there stunned, George and Patti Harrison disembarked from the sedan. George wasn't really very prepossessing at all, but Patti was a vision of beauty, a psychedelic queen who smiled on us and calmed down the two very aggravated Georges. She knew that we were harmless fans come to honour Beatledom, and while she smiled her guileless smile, we felt like we were in the presence of a divine goddess from another reality. Canadian Peter recovered first, and awkwardly handed George Harrison the tape, mumbling something. I followed suit, even more awkwardly giving George my thin booklet, and saying I hoped he would enjoy it.

An invitation inside was not forthcoming, although I believe Patti wanted to ask us all in. We were all so enthralled at meeting George and Patti, awkward as all involved had been, that we decamped and blissfully headed back in the dusk for the bus to Richmond.

Several weeks later, a few members of the entourage went back to pick up the tape. Apparently a record contract wasn't immediately offered, but Canadian Peter did have some good news for me. George Harrison told me to tell you that he really liked your poetry. I was thrilled, even though I now realized that Harrison was a mere, awkward mortal, and I was no longer in his thrall. As a postscript, I note that George Harrison's first solo album, *All Things Must Pass*, had the lyrics printed on the sleeve like poems. I like to fantasize that maybe my booklet had some subtle influence, but that's wild hope and speculation ...

The Beatles in Us

Manuel de Jesús Velázquez León

It was around 1964 or 1965 when I first heard the music of the Beatles. I was a twelve-year-old preteen raised on a farm fifty kilometers from Holguín, Cuba. We were without electricity. Our only connection to the outside world was a yellow battery-operated radio serviced by a wire antenna my younger sister and I strung from the branches of two cedar trees our father had planted to hold the barbed-wire fence protecting Mother's flower garden.

In the midst of a nationalist revolution Cuban radio stations filled their musical programs with bland Cuban music. Most of it was of poor quality. We believed that assessment because many of our best and most popular musicians had fled the country in those years and those exiles were consequently banned from the airwaves. There was an eight p.m. radio program called *Nocturno* that we eagerly awaited. A presenter with a grave, bass voice would introduce the audience to the latest hits, both national and international. One night of their broadcast was dedicated to "romantic" songs. If I recall correctly it was Friday evening. We loved those songs the most.

Since the sun sets fast in my tropical home there is no dusk here. Our farm and its surrounding meadows sank into sudden darkness. Steeped in the Caribbean blackness, lit by the glow of an oil lamp, my sister and I tuned our radio to *Nocturno*. Isolated as we were from the world of foreign culture, we felt lonesome and remote. The music we heard then became a magic path to hope, a constellation that illuminated the invisible horizons of our nights.

I think that first Beatle song we heard was "Love Me Do". Then came "Please Please Me". Later we heard "From Me to You" and "I Want to Hold Your Hand". We felt those songs as though they sang only to us. To Manuel, the Cuban farm boy, and to his eleven-year-old sister. We did not understand most of the lyrics, but that was no barrier to a deep connection. We never saw pictures of the Beatles back then. We simply had to imagine their young faces. But somehow we knew that were like us, that they were singing for us, about us, with us. This is the way we still feel about the Beatles today, in us.

Today, all over Cuba there are hundreds of multi-generational fan clubs dedicated to the music of the sixties. The Beatles in particular occupy a place of honour in this period of my youth, the *Prodigious Decade.*

Imagine Camp

Vanessa Shields

Back in time
I'm 15
At leadership camp
In Orillia

Feeling anything but
Leader-like
Wood crutches hold me up
My calf mangled

I hobble to the back
Of the mess hall
Looking for a
A wall to flower

I feel old
I feel pensive
I wonder at my lesson here
I don't think my purpose is to shine

The talent show ensues
One young performer takes the stage
Cautious yet determined
Piano keys await

Her fingers
She sits
Her skin Snow-White pale
Her hair a massive pile

Of natural curls
Then the notes
Simple and familiar
Imagine there's no heaven

She sings from the heart
Eyes closed and the
Crowd becomes disciples
Of such commitment

That like a gentle breeze
All voices join in her devotion
And everyone knows
The words but I

And just like that
We're elevated
To the zone
Above our heads

A place where change exists
And it does not matter
That I do not know the words
They know me

I join the anthem
In honour of possibility
In honour of peace and in honour
Of making music

That is not afraid of anything

My grandson Talli, a little boy living in Korea, proudly shows me his recently acquired rhinoceros beetle, happily letting it walk the back of his hand. He tells me he hasn't named his insect pet yet. I suggest he call him Ringo. He doesn't like that name. I suggest—John Paul George and Ringo—a sort of portmanteau homage to the band Mick Jagger had once nicknamed 'the four-headed monster'. Talli gets mad. He doesn't like my suggestion. He doesn't get my joke. He's only five and he lives in a land of Gangnam Style at a time of Psy and his ultra-popular video viral horse dance. He doesn't know anything about the Beatles. It's Uncle Sean, not dad Dylan who is the Beatle fan. Uncle Sean who taught Talli how to spit in the street. I say, come to Canada Talli, and bring brother Teo, Grandpa Lee and Uncle Sean will soon have the two of you thinking straight. Unfortunately, by the next time we skype, the poor rhinoceros beetle has perished. Poor John-Paul-George-and-Ringo has passed into beetle paradise. Now son Sean has a son. "Your grandson Cayden falls asleep best when he's listening to Paul McCartney," says Sean. And grandpa cannot help but be pleased by that.

John B. Lee

Author Bios:

Kathleen Abley was born in Liverpool. Too young for the Cavern Club, she recalls how John Lennon would cadge ciggies from her cousin. She lives in London, Ontario.

Julia Baird is John Lennon's half sister. In 2007 she published her memoir *Imagine This - Growing up with my brother John Lennon.* She is now a director of Cavern City Tours in Liverpool.

Kimmy Beach's fifth book, *The Last Temptation of Bond* (The University of Alberta Press, 2013), won the 2014 Tom Fairley Award for Editorial Excellence.

Roger Bell lives in Port McNicoll. The author of several books of poetry, his memoir *Candy Cigarettes, (Black Moss Press, 2010)* relates the story of his childhood in Port Elgin, Ontario.

Roy Bentley's books include *The Trouble with a Short Horse in Montana* (White Pine, 2006) and *Starlight Taxi* (Lynx House, 2013).

Julie Berry lives in the country outside of St. Thomas, Ontario where she writes poetry. She is the author of several collections of poetry,

Ronnie R. Brown lives in Ottawa. Three times short-listed for the Acorn-Plantos People's Poetry Award, her work has appeared in over one hundred magazines and anthologies.

Terry Ann Carter is an internationally recognized haiku and tanka poet. She has won many awards for her Japanese literary forms. Her latest book is *Day Moon Rising, (Black Moss Press 2013)*

Ron Charach is the author of many books of poetry. A widely published author, he is editor of *The Naked Physician,* an anthology of poetry by physicians. He is a psychiatrist with a practice in Toronto.

Robert Cording teaches English and creative writing at College of the Holy Cross in Worcester, Massachusetts, USA. He has published six collections of poems including *Walking with Ruskin (CavanKerry Press, 2010).*

Deborah Cox has previously won several awards for her poetry, including the Dr. William Henry Drummond poetry award. Her first chapbook is entitled *The Outlandishness of Breathing.*

Birgit Elston has won prizes in several Ontario writers' contests for both short fiction and poetry. She lives in Hamilton, Ontario.

Chris Faiers is a Canadian born VN War resister, seminal haiku/haibun, 19 collections, over 100 mags & anthos, Acorn Award, village librarian, coordinator Purdy Country Lit-Fests/ZenRiver Gardens.

Misha Feigin was born and raised in Moscow and known as one of Russia's premier guitarists. Songwriter and winner of the Thomas Merton Poetry Prize in 2000 he immigrated to the United States in 1990. His collection of poems, *The Last Word in Astronomy*, is published by Fleur Publishing.

Marty Gervais is an acclaimed author of several best-selling works. An award-winning poet, photographer, editor, publisher and professor he is also appointed Poet Laureate of Windsor.

Katherine L. Gordon is a rural Ontario poet enjoying an international connect to contemporary poets through her books, anthologies and reviews.

Andreas Gripp is the author of seventeen books of poetry including his latest, *The Breakfast of Birds (Harmonia Press, 2013).* He lives in London, Ontario.

Richard M. Grove (Tai) is an artist, photographer, writer, editor and publisher living in Presqu'il Provincial Park with his wife, Kim. Richard is president of the Canada Cuba Literary Alliance as well as founding president of the Brighton Arts Council, former VP of CAA - Toronto.

Don Gutteridge is the author of forty books. His popular series of mystery novels, published by Simon & Shuster, is set in early Upper Canada. A professor emeritus of Western University, he lives in London, Ontario.

Robert Hilles is a multi-award winning author living in Salt Spring Island, British Columbia. He won the Governor General's Award for Poetry for *Cantos from a Small Room.*

Amber Homeniuk works as an expressive art therapist. She blogs her groovy outfits at *Butane Anvil,* and is kept by a small flock of hens.

Bill Howell one of the original Storm Warning poets has had an award-winning literary career spanning four decades. He lives in Toronto, Ontario.

Laurence Hutchman is a poet living in Oakville. The author of many volumes of poetry, in 2007 he received the Alden Nowlan Award for Excellence in English-language Literary Arts.

Keith Inman is a multi-award winning poet living in the Niagara Peninsula.

I.B. Iskov is the founder of The Ontario Poetry Society—www.theontariopoetrysociety.ca. Her latest poetry collection *In a Wintered Nest,* was published by Serengeti Press, June, 2013.

Paul Jeong is a student living in Korea. "It's Raining" is his first published poem.

Maureen Korp lives in Ottawa. A historian, Dr. Korp has returned to writing after living and working in faraway Pakistan.

Dylan Lee lives in Gungpo City, South Korea. A member of the Ontario Poetry Society, he teaches English and edits and writes text books several of which have been published in Korea.

Manuel de Jesús Velàzquez Leon lives in Holguín, Cuba where he is a professor of values education. The author of several books, in collaboration with John B. Lee, he co-translated *Sweet Cuba: The Building of a Poetic Tradition: 1608-1958* (Hidden Brook Press, 2010).

Sandra Lloyd is a member of the Hamilton Poetry Centre and she is currently pursuing a Masters in Creative Writing at U of T. Her prose and poetry have appeared in many publications.

Hugh MacDonald is an award-winning author and former Poet Laureate of Prince Edward Island. In addition to his poetry, he is also a writer of many popular children's books.

David McGimpsey is a multi-award winning critically acclaimed author, editor, humourist living in Montreal, Quebec. He was a named one of the Top Ten English Language Poets in Canada by CBC.

Bruce Meyer is author of over thirty-six books of poetry, fiction, non-fiction, literary journalism and pedagogy. He is the inaugural Poet Laureate of the City of Barrie, Ont.

Colin Morton was fourteen when the Beatles first came to North America. He began writing poetry a year later. His poetry and fiction have appeared in *Descant, The Fiddlehead, Arc, Grain, The Malahat Review, Ascent,* and *The North American Review.*In 1986 he was the winner of the Archibald Lampman Award for poetry.

Mary Ann Mulhern is a Windsor teacher, poet, and former nun. Her fifth book *Brides in Black,* ws published by Black Moss Press in 2012.

Honey Novick is a singer, songwriter, voice teacher and poet. She lives in Toronto, Ontario.

Robert Priest is a Canadian poet, children's author and singer/songwriter. Priest's plays, novels and songs have earned him awards and recognition in Canadian literary circles with a growing reader/listenership worldwide.

Frances Roberts-Reilly is an award winning poet, writer and filmmaker. Born in England, she came to Canada in 1968.

Denis Robillard teaches high school in Windsor, Ontario. Over 80 of his poems have appeared in small presses and on line magazines across Canada, USA, England and Scotland.

Gary Schatte lives in Chatham, Ontario. A lifelong fan of the Beatles, he had the good fortune to see them in concert in Toronto.

Michael Schatte is one of Canada's premier guitarists. Appearing on the Mike Bullard Show at sixteen, he has written and recorded a number of highly acclaimed CD's with his band, The Michael Schatte Band. His most recent EP *Four Songs, One Apocalypse* was released in 2013.

Susan Evans Shaw is an author and historian living in Hamilton, Ontario.

Vanessa Shields writes and lives with her family in Windsor, Ontario, where The Beatles are often the soundtrack to their after-dinner dance parties.

Laurie Smith is a two-time winner of the Mayor's Awards of Excellence in the Arts for the city of Windsor and the first recipient of the Adele Wiseman Poetry Prize.

Ron Smith is an award-winning poet. He is currently Writer-in-Residence at St. Christopher's School in Richmond, Virginia, where he teaches courses in poetry at the University of Richmond.

Elizabet Stevens has won awards for her poetry, including one from the Maine State Writers' Conference. Her fiction and poetry have been published in newspapers in the Atlantic Region, as well as in literary journals across Canada.

Betsy Struthers lives in Peterborough, Ontario, where she works as a freelance editor. She has published nine books of poetry, three novels and a book of short fiction.

Robert Sward is an American and Canadian poet and novelist. Jack Foley, in his *Introduction to Sward's Collected Poems, 1957–2004* (Black Moss Press, 2004) calls him, "in truth, a citizen, at heart, of both countries."

Mark Tovey is a cognitive scientist, cultural historian, and playwright, with an interest in the history of the Beatles, especially McCartney's solo work.

John Tyndall is the author of several collections of poetry. His most recent publication was *The Fee for Exultation, (Black Moss Press, 2007).* He lives in London, Ontario.

Susan Whelehan has written sixteen picture books for young readers, and poetry for young and old. She is currently writing for the award-winning children's television show *The Big Comfy Couch*. She lives in Toronto.

Mike Wilson is a poet and commercial fisherman living in Port Stanley, Ontario.

John Wing lives in Los Angeles where he makes his living as a standup comedian. He has several collections of poetry to his credit.

Anna Yin was born in China and has lived with her family in Mississauga, Ontario for many years. A frequent contributor to literary magazines, she has also been interviewed on numerous occasions on CBC.

Editor Bio:

John B. Lee is the author of over seventy published books including *The Beatles Landed Laughing in New York.* Seeing the Beatles on Ed Sullivan made him want to be a writer.

In 2005 he was named Poet Laureate of Brantford in perpetuity and in 2010 he was named Poet Laureate of Norfolk County – the only Canadian simultaneous two time poet laureate. In 2007 he was made a member of the Chancellor's Circle of the President's Club of McMaster University and named first recipient of the Souwesto Award for his contribution to literature in his home region of southwestern Ontario. He is the recipient of over sixty prestigious international awards. For his writing he is winner of the $10,000 CBC Literary Award for Poetry, the only two-time recipient of the People's Poetry Award, and 2006 winner of the inaugural Souwesto Orison Writing Award (University of Windsor).

In 2007 he was named winner of the Winston Collins Award for Best Canadian Poem. He is the editor of many anthologies including two best-selling works: *That Sign of Perfection: poems and stories on the game of hockey*, and *Smaller Than God: words of spiritual longing.* His work has appeared internationally in over 500 publications, and has been translated into French, Spanish, Korean and Chinese. He has read his work in nations all over the world including, South Africa, France, Korea, Cuba, Canada and the United States. He has received letters of praise from Nelson Mandela, Desmond Tutu, Australian Poet, Les Murray, and Senator Romeo Dallaire. He has been called "the greatest living poet in English," by poet George Whipple. He lives in Port Dover, Ontario where he works as a full-time author.

Other John B. Lee, HBP, books:

Island on the Wind-Breathed Edge of the Sea
ISBN – 978-1-897475-19-5

In the Muddy Shoes of Morning
ISBN – 978-1-897475-64-5

In This We Hear The Light
ISBN – 978-1-897475-96-6

Sweet Cuba: The Building of a Poetic Tradition: 1608-1958
***Translators* – John B. Lee** and Manuel de Jesús Velázquez León
ISBN – 978-1-897475-53-9

When the Full Moon Comes
***Editor* – John B. Lee** ISBN – 978-1-897475-77-5

Beyond the Seventh Morning
***Editor* – John B. Lee** ISBN – 978-1-897475-95-9

Note: *Type the isbn into the search field of your favorite e-store and you will find any of these fine books or ask your local bookstore to order for you from our distributor,* Ingram.

www.ingramcontent.com/pod-product-compliance
Lightning Source LLC
Chambersburg PA
CBHW082122180726
48291CB00011B/2811
* 9 7 8 1 9 2 7 7 2 5 1 4 6 *